ADMINISTRATION OF VOCATIONAL EDUCATION

About the Author

Dr. Dhirendra Verma [illegible] from the Agra University [illegible] College with a Master of Science degree in 1961. He had been a Rockefeller Foundation [illegible] in [illegible] before leaving [illegible] Vocational Education [illegible] Delhi [illegible] Administration [illegible] with the [illegible] *Social, Economic and Political Change*, 1975.

He worked at Canada's Nova Scotia Institute of Technology as an Assistant Professor in the Department of Medical Laboratory Technology for over 12 years before returning to India in 1978 to join the National Institute of Educational Planning and Administration (NIEPA) at New Delhi, as a Senior Fellow, and supervised vocational education programmes at the national level. Currently, he is associated with the Ministry of Health, State of Kuwait as a Senior Consultant and looks after the training requirements of the medical and paramedical personnel.

He has published numerous research [illegible] issues and problems concerning vocational education in some of the leading international journals of Education. He has served as an UNESCO Consultant, contributing to the vocational component of the ISCED (International Standard Classification of Education) [illegible] in the mid 70s.

About the Author

Dr. Dhirendra Verma (*b.* 1940-) initially graduated from the Agra University (Nainital Campus) with a Master of Science degree in 1961. He had been a Rockefeller Foundation scholar at the National Institute of Virology in Pune before leaving for Canada in 1963 on a student scholarship to pursue further studies at St. Mary's University, Halifax where he acquired an M.Ed. in Technical-Vocational Education, and subsequently a Ph.D. in the Administration of Vocational Education from Dalhousie University. The title of his doctoral thesis was "*Technical-Vocational Education in Canada within the Context of Social, Economic, and Political Change: 1875-1975*".

He worked at Canada's Nova Scotia Institute of Technology as an Assistant Professor in the Department of Medical Laboratory Technology for over 12 years before returning to India in 1978 to join the National Institute of Educational Planning and Administration (NIEPA) at New Delhi as a Senior Fellow, and supervised its vocational education programmes at the national level. Presently, he is associated with the Ministry of Health, State of Kuwait as a Senior Consultant and looks after the training requirements of its medical and paramedical personnel.

He has published numerous research articles on issues and problems confronting vocational education in some of the leading international journals of Education. He has served as an UNESCO Consultant, contributing to the vocational component of its ISCED (International Standard Classification of Education) project in the mid 70s.

ADMINISTRATION OF VOCATIONAL EDUCATION

(A Hand Book)

Dhirendra Verma, Ph.D.
Formerly, Associate Professor, Nova Scotia Institute of Technology, Halifax, N.S., Canada
and
Senior Fellow, National Institute of Educational Planning & Administration (NIEPA), New Delhi, India

CONCEPT PUBLISHING COMPANY, NEW DELHI-110059

ISBN : 81-7022-920-0 (HB)

First Published 2001

Published and Printed by
Ashok Kumar Mittal
Concept Publishing Company
A/15-16, Commercial Block, Mohan Garden
New Delhi-110059 (INDIA)

Phones : 5648039, 5649024
Fax : 091-11-5648053
Email : publishing@conceptpub.com

Dedicated

to

Asha, Sharmila, Resham, Mohan
and Virat

Preface

The increased complexity and variability of our occupational life has resulted in the need to train a vast number of people for skilled operations. There seems to be general agreement that this is a responsibility the educational system should assume. Three trends are noted here:

(i) Initial Occupational Training and Retraining

Increasing automation has intensified the need for members of the labour force not only to be mobile in the geographic sense, but also to be variable in their capacities to shift from one type of job to another. Thus, although suitable skills should be developed in the pre-employment training of young people, certain attitudinal capacities are equally to be desired. Whether or not the general school structure should assume responsibility for training for upgrading, or for retraining for an occupational shift, is at least debatable. This is an age of technicians; the chances are that an ever-increasing proportion of jobs will demand a technical-institute level of training. Should the local school structure be extended beyond the eleventh or twelfth grade or should such further training be provided directly by the government?

(ii) Training Government Workers

There has been a rapid increase in the number of workers employed in government service. Schools have still to respond to the responsibility for providing future government workers with such training as will make their social usefulness as great as possible.

(iii) Training for Service Occupations

The increase in the percentage of the population going into service occupations places challenges on the schools to modify the present patterns of vocational training. In addition, it is claimed that the service occupations make particularly strong demands upon the character phases of education.

Obviously, the best place where such varied types of training could be imparted is the public school—more specifically the vocational school. Administration of such school would call for special skills and abilities, and the administrator would have to be oriented in a certain special way to be successful in his task.

The orientation, which a man brings to the job he is to perform, determines in large measure what he does. Vocational school administration, like any job involving a complex of activities and relationships, can be viewed from many perspectives. Some conceive the job of the administrator by focusing their concern upon the purposes of the institutions and thus adopting functions and methods in terms of this criterion. There are others who observe that organisational purposes can be achieved only as certain critical tasks are performed. To them, the job of the administrator is centered on these tasks. A third group views educational administration largely as a process. Thus, this group visualises administration as being primarily concerned with making arrangements for the implementation of these processes. While yet a fourth group may view leadership as the essence of the job, others maintain that the primary purpose of administration is management and control—getting the most done at least cost.

In a sense all of these groups are right, but in another sense each of them has oversimplified the task of vocational school administration by limiting the perspective from which to view it. No administrator can afford to do this. He must come to his task with the realisation that, since no absolute definition of his job has been made, he will have to define it. This he must do in terms of the realities of the situation in which he works, and finally in terms of what make sense to him, what he can live with.

We are not talking here of the rights and privileges of administration. We are simply saying that no matter what influencing factors play upon the definition of an administrator's task, in the last analysis, the significance of his behaviour is dependent upon what gets done (the job he performs) — what results from his understanding, his values, and his acts. It can be no other way. A man can perform only within the realm of his understandings, his values, and imposing his skills. This he does, first by grasping the essentials of administrative theory and behaviour, and later by continually updating his skills throughout his administrative career.

This book is designed to focus thinking on the job of the administrator in a historical and political perspective as well as from a

perspective of the essential functions and the scope of responsibilities faced by the practising administrator in a vocational setting. It is hoped that this range of consideration will provide the developing administrator with general criteria for job selection and the understanding necessary to retain the position which he selects. Finally, the development of a personalised conceptualisation of vocational school administration will serve as the basis for continued study of the job and lead to the personal satisfactions which are derived from knowing that one has reconciled the expectations of the institution, public and self in a rational manner.

Dhirendra Verma

CONTENTS

1

Technical-Vocational Education : Conceptual Framework

The dramatic rise in youth unemployment and under-employment; the shortage of badly-needed personnel in many technical, semi-professional, and skilled occupations; the retraining and continuing education needs of workers displaced by automation; and the rising demand for new educational opportunities. All these factors during the past two or three decades, have focused public attention on technical-vocational education in a variety of ways. One aspect of this interest in occupationally oriented education is the study of ways by which it could be effectively administered or managed. The purpose of this book is to help achieve that aim. But before attempting that it is essential that concepts on which this type of education is based, be fully understood and the term associated with it, clearly defined.

DEFINING EDUCATION AS A WHOLE

Education, in its broadest sense, may be defined as a process designed to inculcate the knowledge, skills and attitudes necessary to enable individuals to cope effectively with their environment. Its primary purpose is to foster and promote the fullest individual self-realization for all people. Achieving this goal requires understanding of, and commitment to, the proposition that education is a primary instrument for social and economic advancement and human welfare.

The main objective of education is to develop the capacities which will enable each person to manage himself in the most effective manner. The mental powers of people are playing an expanding role in social and economic developments; they are basic to the realization of individual dignity, human progress, and even national survival. To help

every person develop these powers is thus a tremendously important goal of education.

The function of education is not only to enable people to adjust to their environment, but to change the environment when necessary to the end that the greatest and most enduring satisfaction may accrue to each person and to society. The fulfillment of this function will depend largely upon the effectiveness of the educational system in helping each person develop his capacities so that he may make his maximum contribution to society and, in return, reap the full benefits of what society has to offer.

Society makes certain demands of its members. Every normal person is entitled to acquire as his birthright, an education that will enable him to meet the demands which society imposes on him. At least these four aims that relate to the fundamental activities of everyday life seem to be the responsibility of education:

1. To develop the individual as completely as possible,
2. To promote desirable personal-group relationships,
3. To make persons responsive to the welfare of others, and
4. To prepare people for proficiency in their vocations.

The fourth aim implies continuous systematic instruction to develop or further develop the abilities needed for proficiency in the vocation. It makes necessary programmes of instruction for persons of all ages in all communities of the state—those in high school, those who have completed or discontinued their formal education and are preparing to enter the labour market, those already employed who need to upgrade their skills-or learn new ones, and those with special educational handicaps.

DEFINING TECHNICAL-VOCATIONAL EDUCATION

Technical-vocational education may be defined as that part of one's education intended to help one choose an occupation, prepare to enter income generating employment, hold employment, keep abreast of changes in a speciality, secure promotion, or to change occupations. The guiding purpose of technical-vocational education is to develop the competencies needed to enter or advance in a vocation or career.

A vocation is one's work. Every vocation has its economic aspect, the production of goods or services of economic value. The goods or

services may or may not be bought or sold. (There is the possibility of their being bought or sold.) Vocations are the product of a division of labour. The development of vocations increased the amount and quality of goods and services for man. It will continue to increase them. How crude our goods and services would be and how limited the supply of them without the division of labour and the consequent specialization in it—the underlying forces of vocational development.

Psychologists indicate that a man's work is the most important aspect of his life and that nearly all other experiences revolve around it. This would suggest that in meeting the basic needs of people an essential factor is a job, a vocation—one that matches the abilities, aptitudes, and interests of the individual, challenges his abilities, and gives him satisfaction. To the degree that this is true, the individual is able to lead to productive and satisfying life.

Many people fail to see (or to accept the fact) that perhaps most colleges and universities are vocational institutions. They prepare people for vocations—to be teachers, scientists, engineers, doctors, and the like. Vocations which require long and extensive specialized education are professions. Professions are vocations. However, the vocational or technical education with which this book deals is that requiring educational preparation below the level of the baccalaureate degree. The extent to which people make appropriate vocational choices, become vocationally educated, and perform satisfactorily in their vocations will determine the extent to which they will be able to fulfill their proper function in society.

Another element of confusion concerning technical-vocational education has arisen from the tendency of many people to classify as technical-vocational any course dealing with motor or manual skills. Thus, any type of general shop, industrial, or practical arts course is assumed to be technical or vocational. Such courses serve an important purpose, but although they may provide useful pre-vocational exploratory experience, by intent they prepare for no specific vocation and must be considered a part of the programme of broad general education. Whether or not a field of study involves manual skills or verbal understandings, the criterion of distinction should be the central purpose of that work, only if it is directed toward competence in a defined occupation can it be truly said to be vocational.

A word of caution is necessary here. Delimiting technical-vocational education to preparation for specific, defined occupations does not imply that the field is extremely narrow and limited to mastery of only a few

specialized skills. Many fields of technical-vocational education require the development of attitudes, problem-solving abilities, and mastery of a considerable range of information as well as special skills. In fact, a broad programme of technical-vocational education will contribute to the general education of the student, but again, in spite of the claims of some enthusiastic adherents, technical-vocational education is not a substitute for general education any more than general education alone can serve the purpose of technical-vocational education.

RELATION OF GENERAL EDUCATION AND TECHNICAL-VOCATIONAL EDUCATION

General education and technical-vocational education are phases of a single educational process—that of directing forces toward the full realization of the potentials of each person. The education of a person does not take place in separate cells or segments. It is a unified, continuous, life-oriented process which, in alert, active people, goes on until death. There is a distinction between general education and technical-vocational education, and it should be clearly understood by all educational administrators. The programmes are not opposed to each other. Neither of them is to be thought of as *versus* the other, but they are not the same.

It is largely in orientation and purpose that general education and technical-vocational education are different. In general education one learns much that is of use to him in his vocation. General education is needed by *all* persons. It is *general* in the sense that it is the education common to all. The "problems of vocation" are not common to all; they are different from one vocation to another. The term "general education" should be used to include all the education which is not directed toward educating the individual for employment and which applies alike to all persons regardless of their occupational distinction. That such education may contribute to vocational success no one should question. But this does not make of it vocational education.

The *first three* aims of education, listed earlier in this chapter, apply to the education of all persons; their attainment is commonly referred to as "general education". The *fourth* aim is the primary aim of technical-vocational education. However, an effective programme of technical-vocational education must recognize the first three aims which apply to the education of all persons, and it must contribute to the attainment of these aims. Attainment of these three aims rests with all groups of

educators, technical-vocational groups included. If learning is the process by which, one, from his own activity (experience), becomes changed in behaviour, many of the desirable activities necessary to attain the first three aims of education must be continued during one's vocational education.

TECHNICAL-VOCATIONAL EDUCATION IN THE SCHOOL CURRICULUM

Owing to slavery and serfdom in the long centuries preceding Industrial Revolution, technical-vocational education rarely if ever occupied a place in the traditionally respected curriculum of the schools. On the contrary, if given at all, training in commercial and industrial arts took place through apprenticeship outside the regular schools. This sort of training reached a particularly high level of development during the guild system of the late Middle Ages and the Renaissance. In England and later colonial America apprenticeship was the course of instruction not only for the various vocations but often for the various professions as well. Article of apprenticeship generally obligated a master to teach his apprentice two things, the secrets, or "mysteries", of his trade and such items of general education as literacy and morality. As the apprentice usually became a member of his master's household, his department was also subject to his master's oversight.

The advent of the Industrial Revolution shifted production from the home to the factory, from handicraft to power-driven machinery. Such a radical shift in methods of production demanded radical readjustments in trade, vocational, or technical education. The hand worker used to become acquainted with the entire cource of manufacture, from the procurement of raw material to the distribution of the finished product. The machine worker, on the other hand, seldom became acquainted with more than a fraction of the total process of machinofacture. Moreover, in place of a master pledged to oversee his general and moral education, he had for an employer an industrial capitalist who felt no particular obligation to look out for the personal education of his employee.

The exact form of readjustment in technical-vocational education to which the Industrial Revolution pointed did not become evident at once. Slowly, however, two trends began to appear. In the first place, as technical-vocational education ceased to be an incident of production and therefore a responsibility of the producer, it became necessary for the first time to look to the school to take this orphan into its curriculum.

In the second place, since the machines of industry operated on complicated scientific principles and since the economics and politics of industrial capitalism became correspondingly intricate, it became necessary to elevate technical-vocational training to the dignity of a formal school subject.

While these trends were making themselves manifest, the forces of sense realism and materialism were also instigating a new role for work in the curriculum. Educators such as Rousseau, Hecker, Basedow, Pestalozzi, Fellenberg, Froebel, and Dewey tried to revitalize the highly verbal Humanistic curriculum of the seventeenth century by putting greater emphasis on a study of concrete objects or things. All of them believed that the primary root of educational activity lay in the child's instinctive propensities for action. Vocational education had arrived. The term was applied to designate any training whose purpose was to equip individuals to support themselves and contribute to the welfare of society by scientific occupations. It stood against general education, which had the development of the individual in all his human functions in view; and against professional education, which required a much higher and broader preparation and a prolonged period of scientific study. Somewhere in the middle lay the concept of technical education. This was education designed at upper secondary level to prepare middle-level personnel such as technicians, technical supervisors etc. in industrial establishments.

Technical-vocational education in the twentieth century was influenced greatly by the two world wars. World War I was a war of mechanical forces. It was recognized that in order to fight a mechanical war, trained mechanics, technicians, and highly experienced supervisory forces would be needed in addition to troops. The war effort also created and expanded industries. To produce the necessary equipment and supplies, industry required increasing numbers of trained craftsmen. National governments in most industrialized countries prepared themselves to provide the trained manpower.

After the war had been waged for over a year, the wounded men who were of no further value to the armed forces began to return back from the front. The warring nations organized intense efforts to salvage as many of these as possible for civilian life by training those who could not return to their former occupations for new vocations which lay within their remaining power.

The vocational training which was provided was intense, practical, and usually effective. Thousands of disabled soldiers were given the ability to maintain themselves in gainful occupations which were suited

to their impaired physical powers. The training programme was carried out across the entire spectrum of society and everybody became aware of the value of the technical-vocational education applied to a variety of difficult cases. It became apparent that it would be of great benefit if it were generally available to workers of all kinds under normal conditions of peace. When the war ended the public in general was alive to the need of technical-vocational education.

The war was beneficial to technical-vocational education in a number of ways. Apart from the fact that most countries became conscious of the need for vocational education it became clear that:

(a) Adults needed training even after they were employed,
(b) Women could be trained to do men's work,
(c) Supervisors needed to be trained through short, intensive courses, and
(d) Vocational education was a preparation for living needed by all normal individuals rather than a device for keeping youth in school or for taking care of delinquents.

Foreman training was perhaps the largest direct result of vocational education involvement in this war effort.

Technical-vocational education was again called upon for help when Second World War was declared. The circumstances, however, were quite different. Since 1917, the "regular programme" of day, part-time, and evening schools had been in operation, and there was a large pool of trained teachers, supervisors, and administrators of vocational education programmes to spearhead the war production efforts. In addition, thousands of inductees were graduates of technical-vocational programmes and thus possessed the needed competence. A large number of industrial workers were also similarly trained. The efforts of Second World War were largely a matter of expanding existing programmes and marshalling the trained leaders.

During national emergencies everywhere, vocational education has provided leadership to prepare manpower for the country's needs. In many instances, government supervisors and college teacher-educators have gone directly into factories to teach or supervise classes. Most such training programmes were just that—training programmes. They were designed as short-unit courses to train production workers to perform single-skill operations. Colleagues of vocational educators involved with such programmes often equated single-skill training with

vocational education. This explains the roots of many of the stereotypes and misunderstandings that general educators hold of vocational education and educators.

It also affected vocational educators directly in a variety of ways. After Second World War vocational educators were not precise in distinguishing between educational programmes and training programmes. What had been the regular vocational education programmes prior to involvement with war training programmes were often referred to afterward as training programmes. Needless to say, this did not help to bridge the communication gap among vocational educators or between vocational and general educators.

The development of single-unit courses to train production workers in single-skill operations resulted in some trainees of such programmes becoming vocational educators. This was the initial experience of many persons who became high school vocational teachers, administrators, and teacher educators. Their orientation toward vocational education was quite different from those who were involved in regular programmes prior to Second World War and those who entered vocational education after the late 1940s. Many of them perceived vocational teaching as teaching single-skill operations. Relationships between a skill and its theory were not considered important and thus not emphasized in the vocational programmes. Skill development was often taught as an isolated activity and as an end in itself. Fortunately, many of these educators did make the transition to differentiating between skill development and vocational education.

Vocational education has also benefited from experience from national emergencies everywhere in refining its teaching methods. Notwithstanding that the teaching was often narrowly conceived, since the enthusiasm was there, elaborate procedures and techniques were developed to demonstrate and teach skills in these training programmes.

In the post-war period, changes were taking place everywhere in the industrial composition and occupational structure of employment. There was an increase in the number of all types of white collar workers and a sharp drop in the proportion of manual workers, particularly semi-skilled and unskilled. This change from unskilled to skilled blue collar workers, and from blue to white collar workers was caused by a substantial shift in employment from the physical goods-producing industries to the service industries. In the Western world there was also a dramatic decline in agricultural employment due to the mechanization of farming. A wide variety of skill training programmes were introduced in many countries to cope with this situation.

The expansion of technical-vocational education was quite rapid in the 1970s. A large number of technical-vocational institutions were opened all around the world to meet future needs for skilled manpower. Educators everywhere recognized that technical-vocational education must: (i) offer training opportunities to the millions of non-college graduates who would enter the labour market in the 1980s and 1990s; (ii) provide training or retraining for the millions of workers whose skills and technical knowledge must be updated, as well as those whose jobs would disappear due to increasing efficiency, automation, or economic change; (iii) meet the critical needs for highly skilled craftsmen and technicians through education offered during and beyond the high school years; (iv) expand technical-vocational training programmes consistent with employment potential and national income needs; and (v) make educational opportunities equally available to all persons regardless of age, sex, caste, scholastic aptitude, or place of residence.

Nowadays, almost all countries of the world, both developed and developing, provide technical-vocational education to their citizens through modern schools using latest teaching techniques. Anyone who belongs to one of the following categories can avail of the opportunity:

(i) young people in high school preparing to enter the labour market or to become homemakers;
(ii) high school-age youth with academic, socio-economic or other handicaps that prevent them from succeeding in the traditional high school vocational education programme;
(iii) youth and adults who have completed or left high school and are full-time students preparing to enter the labour market; and
(iv) unemployed youth and adults or those working who need training or retraining to achieve employment stability.

Training Methods

Two fundamental methods are used nowadays to train skilled workers for the world of work. In one training is received while working in the production process; the other takes place in some other environment, off-the-job itself. In the former the individual is working on a specific job and simultaneously learning by doing. In the latter he may or may not be employed, but in either case he is trained outside the production process. There is in addition a third method in which both on-the-job and off-the-job trainings are combined. Each of these methods contains an array of discrete sub-groups which may be summarised as follows:

A. Training on-the-job
   1. Informal training.
   2. Formal on-the-job training.
B. Training off-the-job
   1. Public vocational school.
   2. Private vocational school.
   3. Training centre.
   4. Work place or employer.
C. Combined types of training
   1. Formal apprenticeship.
   2. On-the-job training plus related instruction.
   3. Cooperative work training and sandwich courses.

A. *Training on-the-Job*

In its broadest sense training on-the-job involves learning to perform certain tasks while performing on the production line. At the most basic level, a newly hired employee is first shown how to perform the simplest tasks at the work bench. When he succeeds with the easy tasks he is taught how to perform successively more complex operations. While this learning process is going on, the trainee is also working in the production process. To a large degree training on the job is a process of learning by doing on the basis of examinations. Those who do not qualify for the academic are assigned to the vocational programme. In other countries the selection is left to the students, but with advice from guidance counsellors. Where the vocational programme has a good reputation, students who are manually oriented will make a positive choice; elsewhere it is sometimes used as dumping ground for the less qualified academic students. In most cases there are no tuition costs to the students.

The average public vocational school offers training in a number of basic fields such as woodworking, machine shop, welding, electrical work, and auto repair. After some orientation in the various types of work, a student selects an area in which to specialize, though his choice may be limited by the predetermined size of the class. Once the selection is made the student spends a substantial amount of his school time learning about and performing on the specialized equipment in the shop. In addition he takes special courses related to his speciality, such as shop math and blueprint reading. In many countries, especially where the vocational students are so young that they have not completed their basic education, the programme also offers general courses such as

history, literature, and grammar. Vocational school programmes usually run for about three years, but this varies. As part of the public school system, they are administered by the Ministry of Education. Instructors are, therefore, governed by the general civil service rules, but the requirements for teaching shop classes normally include some years of experience in the trade. Depending on the size of the programme, the physical facilities may or may not be independent of the other parts of the school system. A small programme, for example, may be administered as part of a large secondary school where vocational and academic students participate jointly in some courses. It should be noted that the facilities can be used after school, on weekends, and in the evenings for adult vocational training.

More formal programmes will have an instructor whose principal responsibility is to teach groups of trainees to perform a certain job in a safe and efficient manner. Depending on the level of skill the job requires, the training period may be quite short or it may extend a year or two. In numerous instances the programme is self-paced so that each trainee learns as rapidly as he is able. In some of the less formal programmes a supervisor may be responsible for conducting the training. But only in large firms with substantial number of trainees would he spend a large amount of his time in training. In small plants where the number of trainees is also small, a fellow employee may be asked by management to show the new recruit how to do the job. In such situations, the trainee learns a great deal by watching his co-workers.

B. *Training off-the-Job*

Training off-the-job may be offered in a shop class or a regular classroom. The former is used to provide practical experience needed for job training; the latter is used to teach general vocational knowledge.

Because of its broad approach, off-the-job training serves many purposes. It can impart vocational knowledge of immediate use at work, knowledge that must precede work, and knowledge that will be useful over the working life of the individual but is not needed immediately. It can also refresh or sharpen academic skills, such as arithmetic and reading, or related instruction such as shop theory. It can also provide vocational skills that are not taught on the job because it is technically impractical to do so or too expensive because of the production time that is lost in training.

Training off-the-job can take place in a variety of settings: public vocational schools, private schools, and companies.

1. *Public Vocational Schools*: The public vocational school normally is part of the regular school system. In many countries students are assigned to a vocational or college preparatory school.

2. *Private Vocational Schools*: The private vocational school is a profit-making organization that establishes training programmes for occupations that seem to be in great demand and are likely to continue growing. Generally, the courses are geared to students who have completed the legally required years of schooling, and training is limited to a few areas. The facilities include classrooms where related instruction is offered and shops which normally contain rather simple or obsolete machinery. It is assumed that with a broad exposure to a trade, a reasonably able graduate would learn to handle any new machine after a short time on the job. Courses are offered both day and evening, and the tuition charges are generally rather high.

3. *Training Centres*: A training or skill centre offers training in one or more skills to persons who have finished their legally required schooling, either by graduating or dropping out. It may be sponsored by a government agency or, frequently, a group of employers or an industrial association. In addition to shop classes a training centre offers related instruction, but academic courses are unlikely. If sponsored by a government agency, the centre probably offers programmes for occupations that are generally considered in short supply, and the trainees are apt to be broadly trained to meet the needs of a variety of firms and industries. If the centre is sponsored by an industrial group, however, it is likely to offer programmes for occupations specifically needed by the industry, and the trainees will receive rather narrow training. An industrial group would be more apt to finance and sponsor a training centre when the average firm in the industry is not large enough to support its own in-plant programme.

4. *Work Place or Employers*: Training off-the-job may be provided in a firm's own facilities apart from the production process. Depending on the size of the programme, it may be conducted in a special room in the plant or in a separate building on the firm's property. Normally, students in such a programme are assured of a job with the company upon successful completion of the course. The basic shop courses train workers in the use of the firm's equipment, although related instruction may also be offered if it is relevant to the skill required. A large company may set up equipment in a shop class where the trainees get all their experience; other companies may use their regular production equipment for training but at a time when little or no disruption to output occurs.

C. *Combined Types of Training*

A number of programmes combine some aspects of on-the-job and off-the-job training, but there are three basic types: apprenticeship, training on-the-job plus related instruction, and cooperative work training and sandwich courses.

1. *Apprenticeship* : This is a formal programme of predetermined duration which varies with each trade. It combines training at work with formal, mandatory related instruction conducted in the classroom or shop class off the job. There is a prescribed curriculum to be taught in a coherent order with an explicit obligation by the employer to provide training in the tasks necessary to produce a well-rounded journeyman. The employer implicitly commits himself to employ the apprentice when his training is completed. The successful trainee receives a certificate that can be used much like a high school diploma or college degree as evidence that he has attained a certain proficiency in his trade. In a number of countries (the United States and Canada are prime examples), apprentices are generally limited to a relatively small number of skilled crafts referred to as apprenticeable trades. These include the skilled occupations in construction, printing, and machinery. In most other countries around the world the apprenticeship type of training includes not only skilled crafts but also many semi-skilled as well as white-collar occupations. Usually the programmes are supported and developed by employers or employer associations, although there is frequent support by both the government and the trade unions.

In many Western European countries, related classes are often held during scheduled work hours. The apprentices are on released time with pay and thus receive their training on-and off-the-job during the regular work day with compensation for the total time. In the United States, however, the common practice is for apprentices to get related instruction on their own time, usually outside working hours in the evening, although Saturday morning classes are not uncommon.

2. *Training on-the-Job plus Related Instruction* : This type of programme combines some related instruction, given off-the-job, with a specific form of training on-the-job. Many on-the-job programmes, because of the nature of the training or the skills needed for the occupation, require or strongly urge trainees to take specific related courses. In most cases the trainees take such courses on their own time and frequently pay the tuition out of their own funds. In other on-the-job programmes it is recommended or suggested that trainees take some related instruction

but such course work is not integrated with the training on-the-job and is used only as a broadening element in the development of the workers.

3. *Cooperative Work Training and Sandwich Courses* : With young trainees whose formal education is still incomplete, mandatory classroom attendance in public schools combined with training on-the-job is known as cooperative work training. The trainee is still a student and spends more time in a classroom than do adult workers because he must take academic subjects required for a high school diploma. Such programmes involve the cooperation of school and employer inasmuch as the trainee spends part of each day, week, or even month in school and the remaining time at work where he receives training, frequently with pay. The school work is not entirely academic but includes shop courses and related instruction in the area of his occupational interest.

Sandwich courses are a common variation of cooperative work training whereby an adult with a regular full-time job is given time off from work to take vocational courses. They may be geared to a specific trade or job or to upgrading, but in either case they provide additional training to workers who could not afford to give up their jobs or lose time for this instruction.

Major Areas of Technical-Vocational Education

Technical-vocational schools provide varying degree of preparation for many occupations, which may be classified into seven major areas or groups: (1) agricultural education, (2) business education, (3) home economics education, (4) trade and industrial education, (5) distributive education, (6) health occupations education, and (7) technical education. Each of the fields of technical-vocational education listed above has its unique characteristics and patterns of organization. The following brief comments on each can provide no more than meager orientation. The administrator whose school offers work in these areas must be familiar with the very considerable body of literature dealing with specific policies and problems. Without a thorough knowledge of this vast field he will be unable to counsel and work with those of his staff engaged in it.

Agricultural Education

Vocational education in agriculture, as would be expected, is concerned with the development of those skills and understandings necessary for success in farming. Scientific and technological developments in

agriculture have led to a vast expansion of occupations in agricultural production, agricultural farm business management, agricultural mechanics, food processing and other allied agricultural careers. The urbanization of our society has created a growing demand for specialists in ornamental horticulture and landscaping. Programmes in vocational agriculture are most appropriate for schools serving rural areas.

Business Education

About one out of every four students in high school programmes of vocational education is now enrolled in business education curricula. Earlier most vocational schools offered a variety of "commercial" subjects, but the offerings rarely were systematized into viable vocational programmes. Increasing emphasis in business education is being given to cooperative work experience, block-time classes for laboratory work, and simulated office experience. Through cooperative work experience, a very high proportion of students is able to gain placement in full-time positions closely related to the educational preparation provided. Comprehensive curricula have been developed recently to include business data processing, as well as the usual office machines, stenographic-secretarial, bookkeeping, and accounting course offerings. Programmes for post secondary and adult students have been growing rapidly. At the community college level programmes in computing occupations are now widely offered.

Home Economics Education

In addition to vocational home economics, with emphasis on the dual function of preparation for wage-earning careers and family living, home economics courses are designed for exploratory, general education, and pre-vocational purposes. In this connection the curriculum includes experiences in such areas as child development, care and guidance; food selection and preparation with emphasis on nutrition; textiles; clothing selection, care, design, and construction; consumer economics; housing and home furnishing careers; home care of the sick and aged; and other aspects of family living.

Trade and Industrial Education

Trade and industrial education is concerned with preparing students to enter occupations in the skilled trades and in manufacturing or industrial

establishments. In addition to the traditional offerings in construction and machine trades, programmes have been recently developed for a wide variety of maintenance and repair specialities ranging from automotive mechanics to pipe fitting. The occupations covered in this classification are so varied that a realistic programme in vocational education must be adapted to the industries and employment needs of the local community.

Distributive Education

Programmes in distributive education prepare students for careers in distribution and marketing of apparel, general merchandise, and foods, and in various other service areas. Cooperative work experience is an important element of these programmes, whereby students are assigned to a job-training sponsor for work and related study under the supervision of a teacher-coordinator. Many of the programmes in distributive education employ the project method, case analysis, and directed observation prior to cooperative work experience.

Health Occupations Education

The rapidly growing demand for health services has multiplied the need for skilled personnel. In addition to preparing persons as health technicians, practical nurses, and nursing aids, health occupations education includes training of medical office assistants and medical record technicians. Most programmes include cooperative work experience. At the post secondary level an increasing number of two year community colleges have instituted programmes to prepare registered nurses, medical technicians, and other health personnel.

Technical Education

Career opportunities for technicians and specialists have been expanding in many fields, from electronics to computer programming. However, because of the advanced level of preparation required, only a small proportion of the enrolment in technical education is at the higher secondary school level. Technical education programmes have grown rapidly in the two-year community colleges. Because the preparation required for many technical occupations is no less demanding than baccalaureate programmes, there is a problem in recruiting students who

have the necessary background of preparation and aptitude for technical education programmes. In order to provide students with the needed preparation for technical education, pre-technical programmes have been developed in vocational schools, technical institutes, and community colleges. Some programmes extend from higher secondary schools through two years of post secondary preparation. Despite the surplus of engineers which developed during the late 1970s and extended into the 1980s, there exists a shortage of technicians in a variety of fields.

Each of these major fields of technical-vocational education provides several types of educational programes organized primarily for groups of different ages and different vocational needs. The so-called day school programme is for youth regularly enrolled in secondary school and is directed toward providing the competence necessary to enter an occupational field. Part-time programmes for out-of-school youth are primarily concerned with improving the initial adjustment on-the-job for those who have left school. Finally, evening classes for employed adults have as their main purpose the improvement of skills for those who wish to transfer to other occupations. The school administrator must be concerned with this total programme. Although the secondary school is organized primarily for youth, the dynamic and really effective school provides continuous service and is the educational centre for all age groups in the community. The best means of securing the support of the community for youth education is to serve it in all areas of educational activity.

DEFINITION OF TERMS

Words dealing with a particular subject matter often have a specific meaning peculiar to them. The multiplicity of terms in the field of technical-vocational education has produced much confusion in the public mind. To clarify the misconceptions, an exact definition of each term is necessary. The use of these terms in the book will be in the following frame of reference.

I. Programme Definitions

A. *Technical-Vocational Education*

Technical-vocational education may be defined as occupational training for employment. It is often difficult to differentiate between technical and

vocational education. Although there are elements which are common to both, a workable distinction between the two can be made as follows:

1. *Technical Education* : This is education, usually above higher secondary school level but not leading to a degree, directed toward a broad category of occupations in which success is dependent largely upon technical information and understanding of the laws of science and technology as applied to modern design, distribution and service.
2. *Vocational Education* : This is education at higher secondary school or adult level to prepare people for employment directly in trade, industrial, commercial, public health, and resource development. The major emphasis tends to be on the development of psycho-motor, and the related cognitive and affective skills required for successful and efficient operation within the chosen trade.

B. *Manual Training*

This is a programme of education where handwork instruction is based on the theory of formal discipline. The progress of such education includes training the mind through the hand, coordination of hand and eye, appreciation of dignity of labour, and developing the power of observation through the senses.

C. *Co-operative Education*

This is training programme of a type that provides for alternation of study in school with a job in industry or business, the two experiences being so planned and supervised by the school and the employer that each contributes definitely to the student's development in his chosen occupation.

D. *Industrial Arts Education*

This is shopwork of a type which provides general education experiences at the secondary level centered around the industrial and technical aspects of life, and offers orientation in the areas of appreciation, production, consumption, and recreation through actual experiences with materials and goods.

E. *Industrial Education*

This is a generic, all encompassing term used to describe various types of education having to do with the production of material goods and including Industrial Arts, Vocational Education and Technical Education—each having its own aims and objectives.

F. *Apprenticeship*

Apprenticeship training is a series of organized and regulated experiences involving a specific amount of on-the-job and school instruction, designed to impart the skills, trade theory, and related knowledge needed for trade competence, to a learner who is under an agreement with an employer or other responsible body.

II. Institutions

A. *Trade School*

A public or private vocational school offering courses to both young and adults in the skills, technical knowledge, related industrial information and job judgment necessary to success in one or more skilled trades.

B. *Polytechnic, Technical Institute*

An institution offering technical courses at the post-secondary level which are designed to prepare people for positions which lie between the skilled trades and professional university training.

C. *Composite or Comprehensive School*

A school of secondary level offering both general and vocational courses in its programme.

III. Instructional Terms

A. *Curriculum*

An integrated programme of activities, subjects and experiences that are provided for learners under the guidance of a school.

B. *Programme of Studies*

A statement of aims, subject matter and activities arranged in proper sequence to enable individuals registered in a particular programme to reach a specific educational goal.

C. *Operation Sheet*

A document containing directions concerning the performance of a single manipulative task.

D. *Job Sheet*

A document containing directions on how to do, completely and in proper sequence, a number of operations.

E. *Job Analysis*

A detailed listing of duties, operations and skills necessary to perform a clearly defined, specific job, organized into a logical sequence which may be used for teaching, employment or classification.

F. *Trade Analysis*

A detailed, organized listing or breakdown of a trade or occupation for the purpose of determining the skills and operations, tool processes, trade theory, technical and related information which must be learned for the satisfactory performance or practice of the trade or occupation.

G. *Shop*

A place in a school where a particular kind of work is done by students for the purpose of gaining certain experience. The shop is furnished with tools and equipment for carrying out instruction in a specific kind of industrial skill.

H. *Vocational Guidance*

A process designed to aid people to select, to prepare for, to enter, and to progress in an occupation.

SUMMARY

An attempt is made in this chapter to define education in general and technical-vocational education in particular. The former is a process for inculcating knowledge, skills, and attitudes necessary to enable individuals to cope effectively with their environment. The latter is a process for developing the competencies needed to enter or advance in a vocation or career. Both, however, are phases of a single educational process—that of directing forces towards the full realization of the potentials of each person.

The evolution of technical-vocational education is traced from its infancy during the medieval era upto the time it became part of the modern school curriculum. Major training methods and areas of instruction are described. Common terms used in technical-vocational education are defined at the end.

2

Administrative Functions and Processes

Administration can be defined as the coordination of efforts of people toward the achievement of the goals of the organization. Administration, however, has not always been perceived in those terms. Many forces have influenced the image of administration in the last one hundred years. Concepts about the nature of administration have changed, as well as the societal values behind the conceptual developments. These changing values and evolving concepts of administrative functions have had a similar impact and influence for change in the process of administration.

These developments in educational administration raise some searching questions: What are the emerging mental pictures of administration and administrators? What, if anything, is distinctive about educational administration? Is educational administration a science? How shall we look upon processes involved in administration?

It is the purpose of this chapter to examine briefly: (1) the changing conceptions of the work of administration; (2) the changing ideas of the administrators; (3) some unique aspects of educational administration; (4) administrative tasks or functions in education; (5) the processes involved in administration; and (6) some important principles and skills. While a past, present, and future approach to this overview might prove to be highly interesting, this chapter limits itself to a brief backward look, particularly as it relates to the present.

OLD PERSPECTIVES OF ADMINISTRATION

At the beginning of this century, scholars in the field of public administration regarded the governmental processes as consisting of two parts: politics and administration. The distinction between politics and administration has been a subject of considerable debate among

political scientists since that time. One distinction appeared to have been established in these early discussions: The function of administration was to carry out and execute faithfully the policies given to it through the political process, while politics was charged with the responsibility and the formulation and enactment of policy. In the context of educational administration, this says that administration should merely execute and carry out policies, and that the policy making function is to be done by the board of education and the citizens of the community.

Although the arguments continue in some quarters regarding the distinction between policy making and administration, the facts bear out the point that administration plays an increasingly active role in development and advocation of public policy. How can public policy be intelligently formulated apart from concern for administrative experience and know-how? Undoubtedly it was this concern and other problems of practicality that led scholars to espouse the theory of delegation of administrative supervision to administration. These older perspectives of administration were implemented to a large extent in the early history of educational administration when the selectmen, the committee, or the board of education combined policy making and administration in operating schools, leaving very little administration to be executed by the school administrator.

This history and development of the legal structure for administering education reflect a perspective that holds the board of education accountable for the administration of the schools, even to spelling out detailed duties of members and officers of the boards. Comparatively, the laws of the various nations have only recently included specific provisions for delegation of administrative responsibilities in education, certification requirements for school administrators, and delineated duties to be performed.

Leadership Problems

If the concept of a distinction between politics and administration is accepted as practical and feasible, it must be accepted with one important major assumption: that leadership in the advocacy and adoption of important policies and objectives will be provided by the political element in the government, whether in the school system or in municipal, state, or national affairs. Under this concept no provision is made for the administration to advise the political element.

All public affairs, including educational affairs, require determined, alert, timely, intelligent, moral, and politically responsible leadership. The government expects that this type of leadership will emerge as an amalgam of effort by both political officials and professional administrators. Boards of education are expected to employ the kinds of administrators who will provide strong administrative leadership, who will keep the boards continuously informed, and who will provide technical and expert judgment upon which the boards rely for making policy decisions, legislation, and appraisals.

NEW PERSPECTIVES OF ADMINISTRATION

The new perspectives of educational administration are the result of an effort to characterize administration as a science and an administrator as a professional person. There has also been a recognition of the new forces that shape new perspectives in administration—new technologies, population phenomena, ideological conflicts and changes in value systems, knowledge explosion, and the like. The result of these modifiers of the perspectives of administration have led to:

1. Studies and definitions of content dimensions;
2. Analysis and definition of process dimensions;
3. Experimentation and exploration in methodology for training administrators for administration;
4. The utilization of the contributions from the behavioral sciences in studying administrators and administration;
5. A growing trend toward professionalization on the part of practicing administrators evidenced by standards of preparation, ethics, accreditation actions, membership requirements in professional organizations and the like; and
6. A growing body of literature on the subject of administration.

An example of the evidence of change as a result of new perspectives in both business and educational administration is the development in the posture and rigour of college and university programmes focused upon administration. Management development programmes in industry, now becoming common practice, especially in larger industries, are relatively new innovations. Such concepts as full-time administrators, specialization, in-service education for updating and retraining of administrators, selection for training, and the like are relatively new in

education. These and many other evidences of change have resulted in the development of a growing new conception of administration.

PERCEPTIONS OF THE ADMINISTRATOR

The perception of administration is irrevocably tied to the image of the administrator. It has been correctly said, "Administration is people", that is, what we relate to in administration are the persons involved. Therefore, it is fitting that we examine the changes that have taken place in the popular mental picture of the administrator. What is an administrator—manager, boss, dictator, expert, coordinator, leader, generalist, specialist, politician, opportunist? Wherein lies his contribution to administration—as an expert on process, a specialist in instruction, an organizer, an efficiency expert, a human relations authority? Admittedly, the expectations of the administrator are vast and far-flung. His range of responsibilities is wide and varied.

Self-image

Certainly there are several aspects to the image of the administrator. One aspect deals with how others see the administrator; another concept is the self-image. The self-image of the administrator includes (1) the image of himself as he really is; (2) what he perceives others think him to be; and (3) the image of himself he would really like to project. It is not a mere rationalization that the administrator sees himself in relation to the dimensions of administration. He sees himself in relation to the tasks of the job, and in relation to how the tasks are accomplished. His measures of satisfaction or dissatisfaction, success or failure, are tied intimately to the job to be accomplished. He is also perceptive to the various factors, conditions, and environmental complexities that condition his satisfaction and success quotients.

The objective here is not to establish the dimensions of either a corporate or self-image of the administrator, but rather to call attention to the fact that perceptions of the administrator are closely related to the perceptions of administration and that these images are changing and evolving. If a speculation were to be made as to what the administrator should be like, it is the opinion of the author that he would be seen as a "perceptive generalist", a person with broad competencies and interests, including some expertness along defined lines.

UNIQUE ASPECTS OF EDUCATIONAL ADMINISTRATION

Educational administration has much in common with public administration, business administration, and administration in various other organizational settings. Although the insight gained in studies of other types of administration have been most helpful and many of the concepts have proven to have universal applications for all forms of administration, it is also true that educational administration has a certain uniqueness of function and purpose.

It is generally agreed that there are three levels of systems within organization: technical, managerial, and institutional. Whereas much attention has been paid to the managerial level, the technical and institutional levels have been somewhat neglected. It is in these neglected levels that the uniqueness of educational administration is indicated. Campbell, Corbally, and Ramseyer realized this fact and proposed six elements related to the special considerations of educational administration.[1]

These elements relate to: (1) the services which the organization is designed to provide; (2) the nature of the activity; (3) the characteristics of personnel in the organization; and (4) the social appraisal of the function and contribution of the organization. The six elements related to the above dimensions are cruciality to society, public visibility, complexity of function, intimacy of necessary relationships, staff professionalization, and difficulty of appraisal.

Cruciality

What services are expected from an educational organization? What services is the organization designed to provide? How do these services relate to the home, the aspirations of parents for their children, the needs for an intelligent electorate, and other special needs? How crucial are they?

The suggestion here is that education is crucial to the welfare of society and is unique since it is more crucial than many other types of activities. Some indications appear to be pointing to increased cruciality rather than to a diminished importance.

Public Visibility

The nature of the relation of education to the people is noted from several

points of view in this book. Generally speaking, what goes on in a factory manufacturing bolts in a community is far less visible to the people than what goes on in the school, fewer people are involved and fewer people have an interest in bolts than in education.

The high visibility of schools has definite implications for educational administration, and it is probably the major difference between public and private organizations.

Complexity of Function

The functions performed by some organizations are more technical and more complex than others. While not belittling the complexity of any productive organization, it is clear that teaching and learning subsume greater complexity than, say, operating a sawmill; yet they are less complex than operations and functions of a psychiatric ward. One characteristic of school administration is that it involves more than average technical and complex operations. This complexity leads to many organizational and coordinational problems.

Intimacy of Necessary Relationships

Again, on the technical level, the intimacy of operations and the person-to-person contacts in the operations of a school provide a uniqueness to educational administration. The personality and character of the student is often involved. Confidence must be respected, and many fine lines must be drawn between the province of the school and the home, students and teachers, administration and staff, school and community.

Professional Staff

From the point of view of the managerial level, few organizations equal or surpass the school situation with respect to professionalization of staff personnel. Teachers are required to have certain legal qualifications, preparation, and certification. As a consequence, it seems highly probable that administration must pay more attention to personal dispositions of school staff personnel than would the administration of a factory. Matters such as professional values, articulateness in communications, teacher judgments, and the likes serve to contribute to the complexities of administration involving a high degree of professionalization in staff.

Appraisal Difficulties

At the technical level, appraisal in an educational enterprise is more difficult and complex than in most other administrative situations. Appraising the output or success of education requires dealing with many intangibles. It must deal with elusive elements such as what portion of credit can the school claim in the success of a student? How does one determine the impact of the home, community, and other forces on the change of personality in the child? These and other factors relating to appraisal certainly contribute to the uniqueness of educational administration.

ADMINISTRATIVE TASKS

Administration is a process involving a system of inter-woven elements including (1) planning, (2) organization, (3) management, and (4) appraisal and control. A comprehensive understanding of the basic elements of administration is necessary to an appreciation of the tasks in educational administration.

Education is a challenging task. The over-all task of the school is to "educate". Administration in this case is to facilitate teaching and learning. Again, this task represents a system of interrelated sub-tasks. The main operational task areas are:

1. School-community relationships.
2. Curriculum development.
3. Pupil personnel.
4. Staff personnel.
5. Physical facilities.
6. Finance and business management.
7. Organization and structure.

School-community Relationships

Education is largely a public venture. To a marked extent the schools in a community are what some leader, group, or citizens want them to be—no better, no worse. Thus, the harmony of understanding that exists between the schools and citizens becomes very important. Administration is faced with the task of initiating and maintaining an effective programme of school-community relations. The task is not merely one

of "selling" the schools to the people or of "selling" the programme. It involves the establishment of a high level of rapport between the schools and the people, of lifting levels of understanding, and of maintaining a strong commitment to a quality programme of education.

Curriculum Development

This is the task of programme development. Programme development includes those activities in which school personnel and others engage to plan, carry forward, and evaluate instructional experiences. Curriculum development has to do what is taught and how it is taught. It is the duty of the administrator to supervise this process. He must also take the responsibility for arranging for the selection and acquisition of instructional materials. Budget provisions must be made to cover costs of instructional material.

Finally, it becomes the responsibility of the administration to plan and execute a programme of appraisal of instruction. The end products and the results of instruction must be measured against the previously established goals and objectives.

Pupil Personnel

Activities included within the operational area of pupil personnel embrace those services to pupils that supplement regular classroom instruction. Included are such important services such as pupil inventory and organization, pupil accounting, health services, guidance and counselling, testing, control of student behaviour, transportation, psychological service, and the like. All these require planning, organization, staffing, budgeting, coordinating, appraisal, and supervision.

Staff Personnel

Staff personnel is one of the major operational areas in educational administration. It deals with providing the human resources to execute the instructional and service programmes of the institution. Among the specific elements in staff personnel administration are: (1) the development of personnel policies; (2) recruitment of staff—both certificated and non-certificated; (3) screening, testing, and selecting staff people; (4) orientation of new staff; (5) placement and assignment; (6) supervision

and appraisal; (7) personnel records; and (8) various other activities that accompany employer-employee relationships.

Physical Facilities

School buildings, sites, and equipment needed for instruction comprise the major elements in the administrative task of providing for physical facilities. Planning the modern school plant is a major undertaking. It must be functional, flexible, economic, safe, convenient, well-located, well-equipped, well-maintained and so on. Sites have to be carefully chosen and developed. Provisions must be made for parking, practice fields, outdoor sports, and the many other demands made upon school sites. The task also involves the provision for major equipment acquisitions, maintenance, and supervision.

Finance and Business Management

Although closely associated for most purposes and often subsumed under the concepts of business affairs in the school district, finance and business management constitute a two-part administrative task. Recent writers in the field describe the task of school finance as those activities which lead to the receipts of moneys and the funding of the educational enterprise. Business management is described as the task that involves those activities dealing with the expenditures and management of school funds, accounting, and record keeping, and budget-making. The details of business management are described in another chapter.

Organization and Structure

Organization and structure is the task area that has to do with relations of people and systems contrived to achieve defined goals and purposes. Some of the important elements of this task include concepts of formal and informal organization, authority patterns, controlling boards, organization for administration, channels of communication, and participation in administration.

Some of the signs that point to the need for attention to be paid to administrative organization are, for example, (1) a large portion of administrative time and effort spent on "emergencies"; (2) conflicting orders and decisions; (3) unexplained delays in carrying out plans; and (4) sagging morale. These are symptoms of an ailing organizational

structure and a warning that the concepts and principles of administrative organisation should be carefully reviewed.

TENETS OF ADMINISTRATIVE ORGANIZATION

A discussion of tenets, rules, principles, or guidelines for educational administrative organization should be preceded by appropriate reservations and a proper conceptual framework. The reservations should include (1) that the science of administration is very much in its beginning stages; (2) that much of what exists regarding organization has been borrowed from other sources such as the military, business, and industry; and (3) that organization is a task area of administration that has received very little scientific study.

In the field of educational administration, Griffiths, Clark, and others have suggested guidelines for administrative organization. In brief, these are as follows:

1. The role of the administrative staff in an institution is to create an organization within which the decision-making process can operate effectively. The organization should permit decisions to be made as close to the source of effective action as possible.
2. The administrative staff of an educational institution should be organized to provide individual staff members with as much freedom for initiative as is consistent with efficient operation and prudential controls.
3. The administrative functions and the source of decision-making in an institution should be organized to provide the machinery for democratic operation and decentralized decision-making.
4. The purpose of organization is to clarify and distribute responsibility and authority among individuals and groups in an orderly fashion consistent with the purposes of institution.
5. An institution should be organized with a unitary source of decision-making at its head. Authority and responsibility delegated by the chief administrator should result in a unitary pattern of decision-making levels among all subordinates in the institution.
6. The administrative organization, by its very structure should provide for the continuous and cooperative evaluation and redirection of the organization from the point of adequacy and efficiency.[2]

THE ADMINISTRATIVE PROCESS

With the content of educational administration, the jobs to be done (defined earlier in this chapter), it is now necessary to examine the process—the "how" of accomplishment. The key descriptive words in the literature describing the inter-woven elements of the process include planning, organizing, managing, coordinating, decision-making, appraising, controlling, commanding, programming, deliberating, and the like. All authorities seem to agree that there is some kind of sequential order for the elements in the process, but the agreement as to what elements are to be included is much less pronounced.

In the field of educational administration the process is referred to as the "decision-making process" or "administrative process"—both connoting a sequential list of elements, steps or stages. Some of the common elements recognized by the scholars include planning, organizing, coordinating, and appraising. From a review of the literature one gains two important impressions: (1) administration is essentially a way of working with people, and (2) the procedures in the administrative process are organizationally oriented than oriented to the individual.

Although there has been considerable speculation and theoretical analysis of the administrative process, very little in the way of empirical testing of the phenomenon has taken place. From what has been learned it seems fair to say that *the administrative process is the way an organization, through working with people, makes decisions and initiates action to achieve its purposes and goals.*

STAGES IN THE ADMINISTRATIVE PROCESS

Regardless of how the procedure is viewed or defined—decision-making or administrative process—it is a process involving sequential stages. The following is a listing of these stages:

1. Deliberating.
2. Decision-making.
3. Programming.
4. Stimulating.
5. Coordinating.
6. Appraising.

Deliberating

What is the first thing that administration does when faced with a problem? A beginning must be made—one that several steps ahead will result in a hoped for satisfactory solution to the problem, or at least a definite progress toward satisfaction. Deliberation begins at the moment the administration's attention is focused on a problem. Deliberation on what? The dimensions of the problem are determined; facts are gathered on the exact nature of the problem; the gravity of the problem is weighed; and information is collated upon which a decision can be made.

Decision-making

A course of action (a decision) is made based upon due deliberation. Alternatives are weighed and a choice is decided upon. All speculation and serious thinking culminate in a decision. Thus, the major decision is made in the sequence of stages in the administrative process—the decision upon which all minor decisions and other stages of the process depend.

Programming

Once the course of action is decided, it must be planned and programmed for implementation. Some of the elements to be considered in programming are: What resources are available? What planning is necessary? What provisions in the way of budget, equipment, and instructional materials are needed? What staffing may be involved?

Stimulating

This stage involves setting the programme into operation. This is an important stage in the administrative process, particularly for an administration dedicated to wide involvement of people and democratic action. Interest has to be aroused, commitments sought, and action initiated. Motivation must be encouraged, attitudes built, and activities channeled. This is stimulation.

Coordinating

Successful programme implementation must be concerned with harmonious adjustment to the situation and circumstances—coordination. Timing becomes important. Provisions for supplies and

resources must be coordinated. Communications must be channeled. Forces, resources, and actions must be aligned to make their most efficient impact. Poor coordination in the administrative process is sure to have an adverse effect on the implementation phase of the sequences in the procedure.

Appraising

Appraising is the final stage which completes the cycle in the administrative process and deals with the evaluation of all other stages in the process as well as with the net results. It attempts to measure success or failure and the reasons why. Immediate, short, and long-range impact of the action will be stressed. Things learned through the experience will be noted for recollection in the next round of action, and thus the cycle continues.

ADMINISTRATIVE SKILLS

In an overview of images of the work of administration and administrators, administrative functions and processes, and principles of organization, to leave unmentioned the whole area of skills would be a gross oversight. By the same token it is recognized that the subject of skills in administration is deserving of a much more comprehensive treatment than is possible here. While skills are usually identified as accomplishments of individuals, there is some evidence to indicate that administrative teams possess varying degrees of corporate administrative skills.

Why is that under new management some languishing enterprises appear to flourish and become successful? What new skills have been brought into play? What brings about change that results in success in the same situation in which the previous management seemed not to succeed? There are many factors which contribute to success in management, but administrative skills are definitely among them.

A skill is a developed or acquired ability—a special proficiency. There are many kinds of skills necessary in the successful administration of a school system. Three categories of skills seem to be especially pertinent: conceptual, technical and human relation skills.

Conceptual Skills

Conceptual skill has to do with the proficiency of administration to

originate ideas, to sense problems, to think out solutions, and to form opinions. This is a skill that is necessary to do short-and long-range planning, to determine direction, to establish priorities, to make estimates of what is ahead, and to assume a posture of "vision". Conceptual skills make it possible to reduce the "risk factor" to a minimum, or at least to recognize its reality. A wise administration will encourage the development and use of the conceptual skills of individuals on the administrative team, but it will also encourage and make use of the corporate skills and resources of the administrative team working as a group.

Technical Skills

Techniques, practices, and methods in administration are subject to skill development and proficiency measures. Indeed, each stage in the administrative process depends on skill development for effectiveness. For example, the degree of excellence with which the administration effects appraisal depends upon the skill brought to bear in its execution. The success of recruitment and placement of the worker may in part depend upon the skills in which a job specification was perceived and written. The solution to a very important administrative problem may depend upon the skill with which the problem was perceived, understood, and communicated to the board of education.

Among the many elements requiring technical skills are budgeting, planning for instruction, communication, preparing reports, estimating costs, involving persons in the group process, interviewing, organizing meetings, preparing agendas, and the host of technical acts related to administration and supervision. These are skills that must be developed by the administrator as an individual and the board of education as a group.

Human Relations Skills

Human relations skills have to do with getting along successfully with people and eliciting their effective and cooperative efforts and production. It involves proficiency in recognizing and working with persons as individuals. Good human relations skills encourage the individuals not only to produce, but also to grow as an individual and a producer in the process. These skills are related to morale building, satisfaction of the producers and the consumers, mutual confidence and respect, and good interpersonal relations.

This chapter provides a general overview of the administrative processes and functions with special reference to education. A more specific and detailed description of the major functions, particularly those having direct relevance to technical-vocational education, will be provided in subsequent chapters.

SUMMARY

A review of the administrative functions and processes in education, once thought as a combination of art and science, indicates a trend toward the establishment of administration as a science. The image of both administration and the administrator have evolved from comparatively simple concepts to increasingly sophisticated entities. It has been suggested that educational administration has certain elements of distinctiveness in comparison with business and industrial administration.

References

1. Campbell, RF; Corbally, JE; and Ramseyer, JA; *Introduction to Educational Administration* (Boston: Allyn and Bacon, Inc., 1962), p. 81.
2. Griffiths, D.; Clark, DL; Wynn, DR; and Iannaccone, L., *Organizing Schools for Effective Education* (Danville, Ill.: The Interstate Printers & Publishers, Inc., 1962), pp. 71-72.

3

Administrative Methods in Technical-Vocational Education

Administrative methods in technical-vocational education differ from those in general education due to such factors as the interests of the learner, the demands of the world of work, the standards of achievement and performance, the techniques of teaching skills, and the technological changes that are constantly occurring in the economic order. Keeping in mind a few important guiding principles will help the administrator to better serve the needs of both, students and instructors in a technical-vocational institution.

Obviously, no precise specifications for a programme of technical-vocational education can be attempted, but certain general methods have characterized successful programmes. They can be sufficiently defined to serve as guiding principles for other effective programmes of technical-vocational education.

GUIDING PRINCIPLES

1. *The primary purpose of real technical-vocational education is to prepare each student to enter and progress in socially useful employment:* This principle may appear obvious, but it is the essential orientation of a functional programme. This is not to belittle concomitant outcomes of genuine importance of the usefulness of programmes directed to other purposes. Direction and guidance will be derived from the specific definable goal of competence in selected occupations.

The administrator of a technical-vocational institution must always keep remembering that the main objective of vocational education is to develop the competencies needed to enter or advance in a vocation. His institution stands ready to aid individuals in discovering their vocational problems and in developing the specific abilities needed for vocational

success for the sake of the individuals and of society.

2. *Technical-vocational education is a continuous programme directed at providing youth in the secondary school with the initial competence necessary to enter an occupation, and older youth and adults with experience to enable them to progress and improve on the job:* Although this particular discussion is primarily concerned with youth education and the secondary school, technical-vocational education is broadly organized to serve and meet the educational needs of people throughout their occupational life. In fact, some of the most extensive and effective programmes in technical-vocational education have been with out-of-school youth and adults as in the tremendous programme of training carried on during World War II. Many of those who have been doubtful of the ability of the secondary school to provide adequate technical-vocational education in the school setting have failed to recognize that final competency is not postulated or intended. Gaining an initial level of competence that can give youth a foothold in the occupational world is the primary intent, for this initial step or foothold is tremendously important and crucial in the life of any youth. Improvement and progress on the job is often a simpler task from a practical standpoint than securing the job originally.

3. *Technical-vocational education must draw its content of study and the educational experience it provides from analysis of occupations:* This has been perhaps the major distinguishing feature of effective technical-vocational programmes. Techniques for the job analysis of many occupations have been developed, and advisory groups drawn from workers in a given occupation have been extensively consulted. A realistic programme of occupational preparation is not a matter of a programme determined by the judgment of experts, a review of the literature, or philosophical speculation. The approach recommended here may seem narrow to those who forget the basic purpose of technical-vocational education. It should be added, however, that occupational analysis does not limit the range of vocational activities; it is needed to give them direction.

The making of an analysis of an occupation can be compared to the making of an inventory of a store. Just as a list is made of all the goods in the store, so a list is made of all the teaching units of the occupation. The instructional units thus obtained can be used for training purposes in school or out of school. Whatever system of analysis is used, it must be simple and readily understood by those who wish to use it.

The occupational analysis technique is necessary in the training of

technical-vocational training personnel. The occupational elements become habits, and habits are not noticeable to those who have them; therefore it is necessary to analyse the occupation and list the elements so the new instructor will know what to teach. Experienced teachers also gain much from reanalyzing their work from time to time to keep it up-to-date.

The term *job-analysis* has become a catchword in many areas of world activity. It has been misused in attempts to identify activities that are not of an analytical nature. While this analysis technique can be used in analyzing other than industrial occupations, it is designed for identifying instructional units for production purposes, rather than for personnel management.

The analysis technique helps to put system into the teaching of occupations and many other activities. In order to study the analysis procedure in its application to technical-vocational training, it is necessary first to make sure that the workers in industry are understood both as to work assignments and to terms used to identify them. Certain terminology also applies to the analysis technique itself. A major consideration is the development of ability to distinguish the elements of an industrial occupation from the jobs in which they are applied.

The training of technical-vocational teachers goes far beyond the making of the analysis. There remains the need for the study of learning and teaching, for course development, and for other phases of instructional procedures.

Analysis is used in selection and organization of subject matter in successful technical-vocational programmes and in research related to new experimental programmes.

4. *Technical-vocational education should be broad enough to include all of the factors that contribute to occupational adequacy:* Technical-vocational education has been criticised for giving too much attention to the development of skills and not enough to attitudes, related information, satisfactory personal adjustment, and relations with others. All these factors must be recognized and experience in them provided insofar as possible if the programme is to escape the charge of narrowness.

5. *Technical-vocational education must be flexible and dynamic:* Technology and invention continually modify occupations, create new ones, and actually eliminate others; hence a fixed programme, no matter what its adequacy on some given date, cannot remain effective unless it is continually modified to meet the demands of time and change.

6. *Administration must be recognized as a decision-making process:* Administration may be defined as the process by which human action is controlled and directed towards specific ends. This implies decision-making. In the administration of technical-vocational education, it is the process through which, by decision-making and effective direction, programmes are conceived, courses organized, and instruction imparted. The entire process is coordinated in such a way that society will have the skilled help required to produce the goods and services it wants. The role of the administrator, properly conceived in this frame of references, is as a guide in the decision-making process.

A decision is the solution, tentative or permanent, to a problem and therefore, it should be arrived at by the problem-solving method or process. The first step in this process is to have a clear definition of the problem. Once the problem has been identified, the administrator can gather any relevant data, and formulate and review all possible courses of action for solving the problem. There is always more than one possible course of action. After a thoughtful decision has been made as to which is most suitable, more specific planning is necessary as to how the chosen course of action is to be implemented.

7. *The administration of a vocational programme must be based on well-defined policies:* Policies provide guidelines for decision-making. A policy is an overall guide which sets the boundaries within which administrative action will take place. A policy defines the area in which decisions are made but does not provide the administrator with the decision. An effective policy requires interpretation by the administrator. Thus, policies aid the administrator in the decision-making process.

Well-formulated policies are broad but do not require complex interpretation. Policies within an institution should be consistent; that is, they do not conflict with one another.

It must be emphasized that an administrator who undertakes to administer a project of any kind, whether it is in business, industry, or education without a clear policy is on dangerous ground. He is quite likely to find himself involved in contradictory and inconsistent actions that will leave him and his staff in a state of confusion. The function of an established policy is to provide the basis for appropriate and consistent action.

8. *The administrator must ensure that each person involved in a vocational programme has a clear understanding of its objectives and the methods employed to achieve them:* Programme objectives are the goals which provide scope and direction to the school administrator. The objectives of the various departments under his supervision should

complement and supplement overall institutional goals and they should be clearly understood by *all*.

An example of an objective for a computer technology department might be "to provide its students with basic computer skills and elements of computer terminology". This objective provides direction for the department head and supports the overall school goal of providing the society with skilled computer technologists.

The process of familiarizing the instructional and supervisory staff with the objectives of the institution must begin from the very moment the members report for duty. The responsibility rests mainly upon the principal who must plant and nourish in the minds of his associates the ideas and basic concepts for which the institution exists.

The variety of methods available to the administrator who wishes to build an instructional team committed intelligently to the purpose for which his programme exists are as wide as his ingenuity permits. Perhaps the commonest vehicle for this purpose is the staff conference where the administrator has the opportunity to present problems in the framework of the philosophy upon which his programme is based. The best time for holding such assemblies is just before the start of school terms.

Another effective channel for use in building the team is the day-do-day contact with the individuals that compose the group. Many administrators consider it as weakness to take their associates into their confidence in the mutual exploration of thoughts and ideas. This is wrong. The administrator whose office is always open to the department heads or other subordinates for the purpose of discussing problems or evaluating the merits of different instructional techniques, indicates the one who has been successful in building a good team.

These comments, by no means exhaust the ways by which the alert administrator develops in the staff the understanding and acceptance of the purposes for which his institution or programme exists.

9. *The administrator is responsible for the creation of charts of organization and work distribution for the benefit of his staff:* In a teaching establishment, especially in a technical-vocational institution, it is very important that each instructor and supervisor knows the limits of his authority and responsibility. An organization chart is a good means of accomplishing that and also informing others about such relationships. Such a chart does not, by itself, ensure good organization, and neither does it ensure good administration, but helps to visualize the entire structure to determine whether the organization has been logically carried out. It crystallizes thinking and brings out important details which might

otherwise have been overlooked. It also helps to discover hidden weaknesses, such as confused lines of authority and responsibility, duplication of functions, inefficient allocation of personnel, too great a span of control, and lack of intermediate supervisory levels.

The first task in the preparation of a chart of organization is to list the main functions of the institution as a whole and each individual department. Under these main functions, in each case, are placed those subordinate to the main ones, and each minor function is then placed under the subordinate function to which it is related. A chart may be based entirely on the functions performed in the institution and individual department, or on the job titles of the personnel performing the functions, or the two may be combined on one chart. A chart showing the job titles could start with the school administrator, and work down to the departmental heads and instructors, and to clerks, librarians, messengers, and any others that may be employed by the institution.

A chart of organization should be titled and dated; if comments are necessary for clarification, they should be appended. When completed, it should be hung where everyone in the institution may see it. The chart of organization thus indicates to the staff their duties, responsibilities, place in the organization, and their chances of advancement.

Another means for reviewing school organization is the work distribution chart. This chart shows how much time each instructor, supervisor, or any other employee spends on his various activities during the work week. If correctly prepared it can point out such organizational defects as uneven distribution of teaching load, excessive or inadequate specialization of work assignments, and disproportionate use of time for certain activities. It is also helpful in identifying areas in the various departments which are in need of procedural review and revision.

There are two major steps in the preparation of a work distribution chart. The first requires that each staff member fill out a daily task list, which is a simple record of time spent on various major activities throughout the working day. To ensure accurate recording of time spent, the administrator should explain to each employee how his task will be used for organizational analysis and that it is not a personal check on his efficiency or productivity. Furthermore, the employee should understand that he does not need to account for every minute of every day—the emphasis should be on major activities.

Each employee should fill out a daily task list for at least a weak. This is necessary because work volume per day fluctuates, and certain tasks require more time to perform on Mondays than on Fridays. At the end of

a work-week each supervisor or department head summarizes the time spent on all activities by each employee, including himself, in his department. The summary task list for the principal of a technical-vocational institution is presented below to illustrate the point. The time and tasks, however, are specified rather arbitrarily.

Name : Mr. X   Position: Principal   Week: Dec. 3—Dec.8

Task (Job)	Hours
1. *Administration*	15
Enrol students	
Conduct correspondence	
Claim or recommend allowances	
Delegate responsibility	
Enforce discipline	
Attend to student and staff grievances	
2. *Training*	10
Recruit staff	
Conduct and attend conferences	
Prepare and issue notices	
Conduct assemblies	
3. *Student Employment*	5
Meeting with the Guidance Counsellor	
Prepare list of employers	
Prepare a master schedule	
Arrange student interviews	
4. *Public Relations*	5
Address interested groups	
Attend to union business	
Prepare press releases	
Confer with local governing bodies	
5. *Building, Equipment, Supplies and Budget*	5
Confer with the Accounts office	
Approve or raise requisitions	
Arrange for utilities and services	
Maintain building and grounds	
	40

The second step in the preparation of the work distribution chart is a listing of the activities of the institution on a large chart. Employees' names are listed on the top, and each employee's tasks and times, are entered on the chart in appropriate columns. The chart is now ready for analysis. The following questions can be asked:

(i) Is a task needlessly spread out among several employees?
(ii) Is the work evenly distributed?
(iii) Are the skills of each employee being fully utilized?
(iv) Is time being spent on unnecessary tasks?
(v) Is the time spent on various activities reasonable and in line with their importance?
(vi) Are employees performing too many unrelated tasks?

Careful preparation and thoughtful analysis of a work analysis chart is an excellent technique for a study of the organization of an institution of technical-vocational learning. It is of great help to the administrator for mobilizing his staff to the best advantage of his institution.

10. *The administrator should have a clear understanding of the legal structure under which he operates:* The structure of educational administration varies from country to country but in most cases the ultimate authority for educating the citizens is placed in a distinct department of education which is usually headed by a minister. In large countries each state or province has its own department of education which may be totally autonomous or governed by the central administration. Often different educational programmes in a given province have different controlling bodies, *i.e.,* central or provincial. The mode of operation of a particular educational programme may also differ in a province. For example, in some provinces the technical-vocational programmes are operated directly by the provincial department of education, in whole or in part; in others they are operated by private bodies within the provincial framework and receiving provincial grants; yet in others both types exist, often in the same community.

Usually the central grants are paid to provincial departments intimately concerned with a particular course or programme. In most cases, the provincial departments of education receive the grants directly or indirectly and disperse them under the central and provincial provisions but other departments such as department of trade and commerce, labour, or transport may also be involved.

Whatever the case may be, it is imperative that the administrator is well familiar with the structural, jurisdictional, and legal framework under which his institution operates. It is also desirable that he has a working knowledge of the central and provincial statutes, regulations, and schedules that affect his organization. In addition, he should be aware of major judicial decisions and administrative regulations governing technical-vocational education in general, and those which apply to his province, institution, programmes, and community in particular.

If the institution is completely under local control with provincial staff concerned with the legal requirements under which grants are paid then the administrator will need detailed information about the entitlements he may claim for buildings, equipment, personnel, and other items for which subsidies may be available.

11. *The administrator must ensure that his instructors possess recognized competency in their area of instruction:* Teachers of technical-vocational subjects are either occupational specialists with a moderate amount of teacher training or professional teachers with some specialized occupational skills. Regardless of whether they are drawn into vocational teaching from the world of work or from academic institutions, there is one essential qualification which they must possess to succeed in their chosen career. They must be recognized masters in the occupational trade taught by them. This recognition should come not only from the licensing agency for the instruction of that trade but also from his peers in the occupational circle from which he comes. A welding instructor with advance teacher training who fails to teach his students the art of welding is of no use to the institution. And this fact must be kept in mind by the administrator while selecting instructors for his institution.

This does not disregard the fact that there are other qualifications which all vocational teachers should possess. The most important being that they should be morally upright and honest. In addition, they should be able to communicate well with the students and show proficiency in areas such as lesson planning, preparation of teaching aids, student evaluation, and the like.

It is also the responsibility of the administrator to arrange opportunities for periodic industrial exposure for his instructional staff. Technological change and innovation require that teachers of technical-vocational programmes be retrained and their training skills updated as new procedures and processes are developed. This means that the learning process must be viewed as cyclical than linear. Instead of school, then teaching, then retirement, there should be a continuing process of

work and learning. Teachers must learn how to learn and learning must be accepted as a life-long process—not something done while in teacher training college and then forgotten.

It will be most desirable if the administrator allows a period of at least 8 to 10 weeks of industrial exposure to all teachers by rotation every third year of their teaching career. However, it would depend on the nature of vocation and the total time available for training. The teachers should be placed in an industry in order to enable them to become familiar with the latest technological innovations in their instructional field. Functioning in a different environment will be a refreshing and morale-boosting exercise for them and, on their return, they are sure to teach more skilfully and with renewed vigour.

As to the curriculum required for the vocational teacher preparation it is suggested that it should have three distinct components: basic education, major, and supplemental. Ideally, the entire teacher training programme should be of two year's duration after the first university degree. The college work in these two years should include courses of the three components as identified above. Probably what the prototype undergraduate teacher education programme (leading to a B. Ed. degree) for teachers of technical-vocational subjects should include is shown in Figure 3.1.

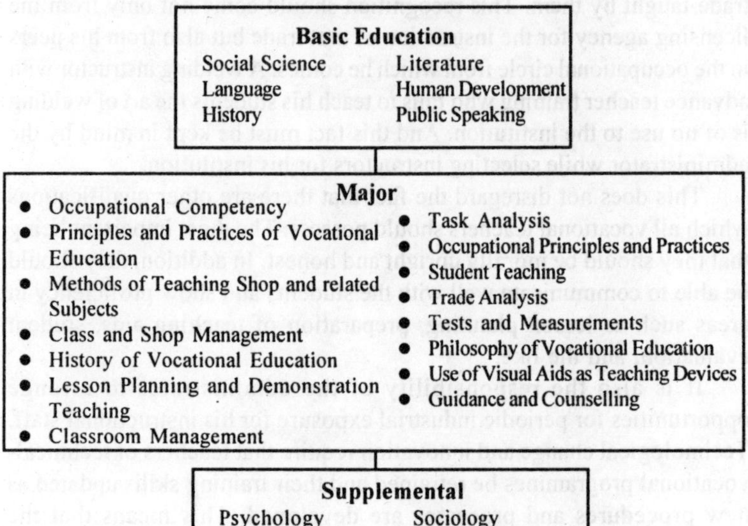

Fig. 3.1: The Vocational Teacher Preparation Curriculum

The administrator should, at all times, be alert in identifying teachers who show evidence of diligent and industrious behaviour. He should help them upgrade themselves academically. The area of coordination and supervision becomes the "first" step in producing future administrators for technical-vocational education. The M.Ed. degree should emphasize this concern through the following course work:

- Introduction to School Administration
- Curriculum Development in the Secondary School
- Administration and Supervision of Vocational and Technical Education
- Curriculum and Materials for Technical-Vocational Education
- Organization and Teaching of Part-Time Cooperative Programmes
- Current Concepts of Technical-Vocational Education
- Research in Technical-Vocational Education: Survey and Methods
- Theories of Learning, Development and Measurement
- Educational Processes for Career Development Programmes
- Structure of Business and Industry
- Master's Project in Technical-Vocational Supervision

  or
- Master's Thesis Study
- Electives as approved by the Department awarding the degree

Outstanding and academically talented vocational educators may be encouraged to aim still higher by pursuing a doctoral level degree in technical-vocational education. The advanced degree should assure the development of a "new breed" of leadership for occupational education with options in administration, research and college teaching. This leader for tomorrow must use the knowledge of the various social and behavioral sciences and perform the function of translating this knowledge into operation. He needs an understanding of the disciplines of the behavioural sciences, including sociology, psychology, and economics so as to be able to integrate research from these fields for the needs of technical-vocational education.

12. *The administrator must, at all times, maintain strong links with industry to ensure that the skill needs of industry are identified and met through the programmes offered at his institution:* There is general unanimity among educators and industry leaders regarding the

desirability and mutual benefits to be derived through cooperative effort in the development and conduct of the vocational and technical education programme offerings of local schools and school systems. Employers can give desired training facilities, reduce their own training costs, and participate in the development of present and future employees. Labour gains a voice in the development of workers and in the development of training programmes which meet the needs of members of their specific groups. The schools benefit by offering courses of instruction and training programmes attuned to the needs of industry and labour, and therefore, play a more meaningful role in the community which, hopefully, provides a broad base of community support for technical-vocational education.

When education and industry ignore each other or fail actively to cooperate, the inevitable result is the school turning out unqualified workers and industry suffering skilled manpower shortages, the students and community are cheated while industry is forced to engage in expensive in-plant training or be satisfied with untrained workers giving low-grade performance. The cost is passed on to the public who thus pays twice—once for ineffective schools and again for the expense of ineffectively trained workmen in industry. The effect on a country's manpower development and utilization efforts is not only negative, but, when allowed to persist, disastrous.

While the literature concerning industry-education cooperation recommends and is almost entirely concerned with the use of formally organized advisory committees to achieve the desired cooperative participation of industry in technical-vocational education, there is an occasional reference to the utilization of specially assigned school staff for industry-liaison purposes, and that cooperation may be effected through informal arrangements between industry and school representatives. The close working relationships thus developed through carefully structured and properly managed industry-education committees, do result in overcoming many of the misunderstanding which sometimes arise between educators and representatives of industry.

A variety of factors motivate industry people to participate and involve themselves in technical-vocational education programmes in their communities. They recognize that their own business interests can be advanced through effecting improvements in the quality and quantity of technical-vocational education. At the same time an outlet is provided for the discharge of civic responsibility which can produce highly satisfying public recognition. Specifically, industry people and their local groups offer their cooperation, counsel, and participation in technical-vocational education programmes because they:

(i) Would like to have the school assume, as much as possible, the burden of initial entry training of new employees.

(ii) Would like to have a reliable source for continuing supply of well-educated and well-trained new employees in order to eliminate many of their recruitment and selection problems.

(iii) Would like the prestige that accrues to the industry as a result of having a programme in the schools.

(iv) Consider their work with schools as fulfilling a civic and community public service responsibility.

(v) May satisfy their desire to be considered altruistic and philanthropic by providing scholarships, prizes, awards and financial aid directly to individual students.

(vi) Desire to take tax advantage benefits that may result from financially supporting occupational education programmes.

Recognition of these motivation factors can provide administrators innumerable clues for developing participation and involvement of industry people in school programmes.

Another advantage that accrues from involving industry in school's affairs is that the administrator is able to attract desirable candidates to enrol in the school's training programmes. Interesting and attracting qualified students to register in a specific vocational education programme presents as many problems to educational administrators as are faced by employers in recruiting qualified applicants for jobs in industry. The fact that jobs may be plentiful and that the earnings may be excellent is no assurance that there will be either a sufficient number of applicants for the school programmes or for industry's plants and offices. The reasons for this situation are many, including the public's attitude toward technical-vocational education as well as "blue-collar" employment.

Industry leaders and vocational educators, both at the high school and post-high school levels, have long recognized their mutuality of interest in helping each other to improve their respective "image" in order to recruit quantitatively and qualitatively. It has been recognized that without this mutuality of interest any amount of instructional and administrative staff time, as well as the time and effort expended by industry people, would be meaningless. Thus, every opportunity and every activity which can possibly contribute to a more knowledgeable public concerning technical-vocational education and the world of work must be utilized by the school administrator and by industry if such

educational programmes are to attract students and have a substantial role in education. Some activities in the realm of industry-education cooperation connected with counselling and recruitment of students for technical-vocational schools are briefly described below:

(i) Local trade associations or Chamber of Commerce provide industry representatives to speak about occupational and career opportunities offered by the particular industry to civic club meetings, and career-day conferences at school.

(ii) Production and distribution of specific occupational career literature, motion pictures, and a variety of visual aids, primarily by national trade associations, but frequently with financial assistance from their affiliated local groups.

(iii) Special scholarships are offered by numerous trade associations and labour organizations as a means of promoting and publicizing the career opportunities of their particular industry, profession or company.

(iv) Prizes and awards to outstanding technical-vocational students is another phase of the growing awareness on the part of industry people that the earlier they get their career opportunities message to students, the more likely the chances are of attracting young people into their industry.

(v) Many technical-vocational institutions conduct such public relations activities as fashion shows by the needle trades students, exhibits of students work in department stores, public galleries and auditoriums.

(vi) Plant tours for students are frequently arranged by technical-vocational teachers in order to supplement instructional programmes by providing students with a better understanding of how industry operates, and to see the equipment and processes about which they have been reading and studying. Despite the fact that plant and office operations are interrupted, employers cooperate with the schools because they recognize the consumer public relations value of such visits, as well as the possibility of helping to recruit students into school programmes and into their companies as employees.

(vii) The Career Day Conference is an extremely popular technique of school guidance counsellors. The programmes are arranged so that students indicate some particular industry or career area in which they are interested and for which the counsellor has

pre-arranged an industry speaker or groups of speakers. Usually one or two days during the school year are set aside for this purpose.

There is yet another area in which the administrator can turn to industry for help. This relates to curriculum development. The process of developing vocational and technical education curricula, courses of study, and instructional material is a continuous and time-consuming job for curriculum specialists. They and other responsible educators must possess an intimate knowledge of specific industry and occupational job entry requirements. Industry can contribute to the process in various ways:

(i) Provide job analysis and employment entry requirements through the medium of manpower and skill needs surveys conducted jointly by school and employment service manpower specialists.
(ii) Provide job analysis information developed by individual employers in a particular industry.
(iii) Assist educators in developing and revising curricula by providing consultants.
(iv) Develop curriculum, course of study and instructional literature through educational committees of national and local employer associations and labour organizations, and disseminate this information to national, regional and local educators.
(v) Serving on advisory committees to review curricula and courses of study as developed by the educators in order to assure suitability in terms of industry requirements, and to suggest revisions.

The development of an occupational education curriculum leads to the related problems of selecting instructors, determining shop and laboratory equipment needs, and considering the type of student to be enrolled in the programme. Industry can be of assistance in the following ways:

(i) Industry can point out the type of equipment needed for a vocational education programme and frequently arrange for donation, loan or special purchase price of equipment as well as shop or laboratory supplies.
(ii) Industry may be asked to suggest the type of student who should be recruited for the vocational and technical school programme in terms of educational background and the job

requirements which must be met upon the completion of the programme, but does not participate in the actual student selection process.

(iii) Industry is frequently called upon by educators to assist in recruiting instructors, but selection is made by the school. Industry can provide opportunities for instructors to up-grade their knowledge and skills.

These are only some of the ways in which industry can help the administrator. He can think of many more but all this can only happen if he maintains cordial relations with representatives of business and commerce operating in his community.

13. *In-school technical-vocational education should be offered in the light of adequate vocational guidance:* Generally speaking, guidance is the process of helping an individual understand himself and his world. Vocational guidance, more specifically, is the assistance given in choosing, preparing for, entering upon, and making progress in an occupation. In its broadest sense all guidance is vocational to a certain degree because it is difficult to separate kinds of guidance into discrete categories.

Collectively, guidance activities amount to something distinguishable from classroom teaching, although good classroom teaching makes frequent use of guidance services. On the other hand, guidance involves special procedures which classroom teachers find difficult to employ without the know-how and assistance of trained guidance personnel. This is especially true in the institutions of technical-vocational learning as these institutions cater to the manpower needs of our technological society. In the past fifty years our society has witnessed tremendous technological change which has had considerable impact on the structure of employment and the economy. Indications are that these changes will continue at a pace equal to, if not greater than, their current rate. The challenge for guidance personnel is not only to keep abreast of those changes, but to be innovative in their approach to finding ways of helping students find their proper vocations. Obviously, this calls for having a professional guidance counsellor on the school staff who is attuned to the needs of workers and employers alike in our constantly changing world of work.

The special functions of the vocational guidance programme are described as follows:

(i) The *appraisal* service, which is designed to collect, analyze,

and use a variety of objective and subjective personal, social and psychological data about each student for the purpose of better understanding him as well as helping him to understand himself.

(ii) An *informational* service, which is designed to provide students with a greater knowledge of educational, vocational and social opportunities so that they may make better informed choices and decisions in an increasingly complex society.

(iii) The *counselling* service, which is designed to facilitate self-understanding and development through didactic or small-group relationships. This facilitates decision-making.

(iv) A *planning, placement* and *follow-up* service, which is designed to assist the student in selecting and utilizing opportunities within the school and labour market that will enhance growth in his chosen occupation.

It is true that some aspects of these services have been provided in schools without an organized programme or trained personnel, but usually such efforts are too incidental to be effective.

In order to make a counselling programme work, the administrator must provide leadership for developing:

(a) A written statement of goals and purpose of the guidance programme and its relationship to the total school programme.
(b) An organizational plan for guidance that is consistent with its goals.
(c) A job description for guidance positions.
(d) Policy statement about the programme.

He must also interpret the programme to others, see that qualified personnel are selected and provide for the evaluation of the programme at regular intervals. He must lead in making known staff and facilities needs for the guidance programme.

As needs change, the programme may also need to change. This may mean changing the roles and functions of members of the guidance team. Evaluation should point the way for whatever adjustments are needed. Such evaluation could indicate need for in-service education of members of the guidance team and new orientation for students.

14. *Space, time and equipment must be adequate to instruction upto the desired level of performance.* The training of students to less

than acceptable standards of space, size, and equipment often brings discredit to institution, no matter how sound the instructional programme is in its content and delivery. The administrator should never lose sight of this fact. Space here refers to the size of workshops, laboratories and classrooms; time to the actual hours of instruction required for a specified course and; equipment to the kind in ordinary use in the trade discipline to be taught.

Traditionally, vocational facilities have been large, unit shops or laboratories, with equipment that replicated that found in business or industry. By necessity, most trade offerings require more than one floor of space vertically, and almost twice or thrice of what is required for an ordinary classroom on the ground level. The administrator must ensure that adequate space is available for a particular programme especially when it is the basic requirement to meet occupational standards. If it is not possible, then the course should not be introduced. The same could be said of the time factor as well. Often general education courses offered in technical-vocational institutions demand more time at the expense of occupational courses. If the time necessary to have the students brought upto the standards of entrance required by the trade cannot be found then the offering must wait till the problem is resolved.

Equipment poses problems of a different nature. The first problem that arises when new programmes are instituted is whether to equip a machine shop or laboratory to the standard of the *best* that exists in the territory to be served, the *average* (if this could be determined), or the *barest minimum*. There will probably never be complete agreement on this point, but there remains a general understanding that the workshop or laboratory set-up is at least as good as what the trainee will find at his place of employment after graduation.

The other problem, often faced by the administrator, is how to persuade authorities to allow discarding of expensive but obsolete equipment. It is a known fact that publicly supported institutions can never match industry when it comes to expenditure on latest, state-of-the-art equipment and machinery. Nevertheless, sufficient funds must be kept aside to update the equipment so that it can match at least what exists in an average size business establishment.

In addition to providing adequate instructional environment, the administrator should strive toward providing employees with the proper work environment. This includes planning for office space for instructors, office furniture and equipment, and spatial conditioning factors such as lighting, colour, sound and air. It is a challenge for the administrator to

bring these together in such a way so that maximum productivity can be obtained while also maximizing employee comfort.

15. *Technical-vocational education should be designed for students of all ability levels:* Special attention should be given to the slow learner and the potential dropout. In many cases the right kind of technical or vocational programme can hold the student's interest and develop in him a desire to obtain enough skills to work successfully. Enriched programmes for the great average group of students should also be developed. Special programmes for the superior students, built around research, experimentation, and problem-solving should be emphasized.

16. *The administrator should take an active interest in the training of apprentices:* A sound apprenticeship programme is an integral component of technical-vocational education. Occupations have become increasingly specialized in huge, complex industrial and business establishments and require scientific and technological information for their satisfactory performance. Apprenticeship and learning by direct experience are important elements in mastering technical-vocational skills, and will continue to be.

The basic problem of developing an effective modern apprenticeship programme is that of creating, under modern conditions, as close approximation as possible of the best type of medieval craft apprenticeship. The essence of the best type of craft apprenticeship was the three fold function of the master craftsman. He was at once employer, representative of labour, and teacher. These functions have been separated and for the most part sharply segregated since the rise of modern industry. The problem, therefore, is to bring together again in an effective unity these three functions. This is where the administrator can play an important role.

The administrator may go as far as his ingenuity permits him to make apprenticeship a successful programme. The most feasible plan seems to be the establishment of apprenticeship committees that are representative of employer, labour, and the school. With such a plan in operation each element of the enterprise can make its appropriate contribution to the proper training of the apprentice.

Apprenticeship varies in its practice and effectiveness in the three major types of trades, namely the factory, the building and the repair trades. Conditions in the factory and repair trades are generally more stable and, therefore, more favourable to successful apprenticeship programmes than they are in the building trades. The most difficult problems are found in building trades programmes because of the seasonal

character of the work, the variety and rapid changing of operation and the reluctance of contractors to employ apprentices. In all cases the school administrator can and should play an important role in the training of apprentices.

17. *Technical-vocational programmes should be developed according to the needs and resources of the community served:* Perhaps the most important function of the administrator of technical-vocational education is the development of programmes that adequately meet local needs. These needs usually involve both the non-vocational and the vocational phases of education—a fact that the administrator must keep in mind while in the process of developing instructional programmes for his institution.

The first step to be taken by the administrator in the development of technical-vocational programmes is to obtain the cooperation of local labour leaders, employers and state technical-vocational education officials. His next step is, with the aid of the cooperating agencies, to make a thorough vocational survey of the community to ascertain as accurately as possible the occupational training needs that can appropriately be met by his institution. This survey may result in making use of all the tested means of meeting such needs and may include evening classes, part-time classes of two or three types, and day trade classes for a number of trades; or it may indicate a need for only two or three types of classes. The programme adopted should so far as possible be the result of full agreement with all agencies concerned. Likewise, the courses should be developed by agreement with the three agencies most concerned and, in addition, the elected leaders of the community.

Another technique in serving the community is through advisory councils or boards. Persons who possess knowledge by virtue of occupational experience or who are in a leadership role or a position of power are asked to join a group to help plan, guide and implement technical-vocational programmes. These boards may be asked to address themselves to many of the concerns raised in the community surveys. The advisory committee could be asked to make recommendations concerning training needs, course content, instructor qualifications, programme evaluation, student recruitment, and counselling of students.

18. *The training strategy adopted by the administrator for his institution must recognize the demographic changes, technological developments and economic shift taking place in the society:* Technological change has the potential to provide substantial benefits to the population, yet change of any sort poses problems and questions

not only for industry, but for government and the people it has been elected to represent. Changes in the structure of employment, in the nature of work, in the relationship between school, work and leisure are expected regardless of whether technological advances are adopted. A decision to ignore technological advances would change our society as surely as a decision to accept them. Views as to the net impact of new technologies are varied but they all point out that technological changes will continue at a rapid pace and the transitions from school to work and from job to job, seldom simple, will become increasingly complex.

Just as the inevitable fact of change is one identifiable element of society in the "Information Age", so, there are other changes that can be predicted with considerable certainty. The first concerns demographics: population in most countries is aging thanks to better health care, and the percentage of available workers in the middle-aged and older brackets is increasing. This means that we cannot depend solely on young graduates to meet the demand for new skills in the work place. Any changes in our system must take this into account. There will be a need to give adult workers the opportunity to learn, train, and retrain whether at home, on the job, in educational institutions, or through community centres. We will not be able to depend on recent graduates to meet the demand for new skills as we have tended to do in the past.

The second change that can be predicted is that the industrial and occupational shape of the workforce will change. We are moving from a resource and manufacturing-based economy to a service-based economy and this movement will continue. The nature of those service jobs will also change—the emphasis will be on services that are exportable, which means they are vulnerable to institutional competition and new technology. Many of the service jobs of the future will be cerebral—ultimately skilled minds, not skilled hands, will determine the value of our services to the market-place.

Technological change will be accompanied by organizational change; how we do things will be as important as what we do. There is a move towards a less regimented and hierarchial form of work organization. Instead of having narrowly specialized individual tasks, people will perform a range of functions using multiple broad skills and increasing levels of self-commitment and personal judgment. Again, the demand will be for workers who can think and learn to adapt.

In order to help our students benefit from technological change and to adapt to its complications we, as administrators, have to make certain changes in our education and training system. These changes, which

essentially relate to changes in attitude, are: the attainment of high generic, rather than highly specialized skill levels; the acceptance of learning as a life-long process; and the realization that training is an investment in the future. These attitudinal changes, coupled with corresponding changes in the training programmes will ensure that local companies and foreign investors have a pool of literate, broadly educated, and skilled talent from which to recruit staff. Skill requirements are not solely demand driven, they are also supply driven—a fact that is often ignored when planning for new skill training is undertaken.

The decision to avoid education and skills upgrading not only deters present investment, it also discourages future investment. This is particularly true in the industrialized world; in which wage resource, and location consideration can be equalled in a variety of centres and in which the existence of a pool of well-educated and flexible employees can determine the site for future and present investment. A shortage of skilled workers lowers productivity because companies must wait until such workers become available or they must relocate to areas with an existing pool of skilled workers. Employees will find other alternatives if educated workers are not available. They will invest in labour-replacing rather than labour supplementing technologies or they will open branches overseas.

19. *A good public relations programme is crucial to the success of technical-vocational programmes:* A modern public relations programme for a technical-vocational school is the sum total of all the activities undertaken in such a way as to bring the public into such close, active touch with the school, its programmes, and its various activities that real public understanding is developed and public support is gained. Although desired for any educational programme it is absolutely essential for the success of programmes in technical-vocational education as its graduates will be looking for gainful employment soon after completing their courses. The more the employers know about these graduates the better it is.

The administrator who has studied the community and its youth and planned with the community for its youth has in those processes used the most fundamental techniques available for attaining the ends of a good public relations programme. As an aspect of those processes, however, it is necessary to keep the community informed concerning the activities of the school and those who plan with it. Keeping the community informed is a part of democratic administration that serves to aid the community in planning, developing, and evaluating the most effective

programmes of technical-vocational education for its youth.

The basic reason for developing a good public relations programme should be to speed up the rate at which the institution can advance from its present level toward being a better institution. The assumption is that the best rate of progress will be reached and maintained when it results from the joint efforts of interested laymen and the leadership of its schools. Efforts to improve the institution made by the public without good educational leadership will be halting and sporadic. Efforts made by educational leaders that do not involve the public cannot succeed because the public will not support leaders or programmes that it no longer understands. Listed below are some practical and timely hints for administrators to obtain the support and cooperation of the community:

(i) Establish a personal acquaintance with many individuals in the community, particularly through informal, friendly contacts.
(ii) Participate in activities pertinent to religious services, business matters, industrial problems, recreational pursuits, and other affairs incident to the life of a responsible citizen.
(iii) Take part regularly in at least one local civil organization.
iv) Establish harmonious relations with the press, radio, TV and other public information agencies.
(v) Keep the community informed—through news releases, speeches casual contacts and other such means—of what the school is doing and what it needs.
(vi) Invite laymen to participate in cooperative planning to improve the institution, always welcoming suggestions from those that do not take an active part.
(vii) Urge staff members and students to tell people in the community what the institution is accomplishing and planning.
(viii) Collaborate with other community leaders, explaining how cooperation between the institution and their groups or organizations may enhance educational opportunities for youth and, in turn, yield benefit to the community.
(ix) Adapt speech and activities to a mode that is readily understood by the various individuals and groups with whom you associate and communicate.
(x) Carefully prepare illustrative material which is so varied that it will appeal to different groups of people. Pictures, charts and graphs, dramatizations, stories and community celebrations are

examples of mediums that may be effective in a programme designed for the general public. Usually the greater the variety of these, the more effective the programme will be . Repetition in varied forms is a pattern which business and industry have used with such great success that the schools may well follow their example.

20. *The administrator owes it to his institution and community to maintain proper relations with the board of education:* In many countries, local citizens of any community can influence and control the local educational institutions through their board of education. In others, there is nothing to correspond to such local boards. In some countries the local "council" has practically nothing to say about staff, programmes, policies or practices. The head of the local school and his staff operate the school under the direction of a state authority. The profession moves into the community and conducts the school as it thinks best on the theory that technical and professional matters ought to be decided and handled entirely by the professional staff, which is not required to get local approval of basic policies.

Where the boards of education exist, they represent the people of the state in their exercise of local public schools. Within the broad framework established by the state, the local board responds to the community and provides the kinds of school, in its judgment, that the community wants and can afford. The board has the final legal authority for management of nearly every phase of school operation.

As the educational leader of the community, the administrator is responsible for building an alert and informed public opinion that will support and even demand effective schools. If they are properly informed, his two greatest allies in this enterprise will be the board and the instructional staff. Hence, the administrator should spend much of his time with both in developing the educational programmes. Members of the board cannot be expected to make wise decisions unless they have had an opportunity to study all the facts and issues involved. Many administrators find that they can best inform board members by spending time with them individually; others prefer to present oral and written reports at one time and in one manner to the whole board. Skilful administrators do not press for decisions or determination of policies by the board until the members have acquired seasoned insights into the issues involved. A premature decision may block the progress of a training programme, whereas, a board can move steadily forward in successive

short steps so long as it moves with complete understanding. As new members come on to the board of education, it is necessary for the administrator and other members of the board to acquaint them as soon as possible with the educational programme as well as with their duties and responsibilities.

Most boards today serve almost exclusively as legislative bodies, adopting major policies. The administrator assumes the responsibility for policy execution. Each needs the counsel and advice of the other in carrying out these functions. The complete understanding of the relationship between the administrator and the board should never be left to chance. The duties, responsibilities, and functional relationship of the two should be clarified at the time the administrator is hired, and if written rules and regulations have not already been prepared, this should be, in a cooperative manner, done at the earliest convenience.

The ultimate success and standing of a school system are probably dependent on nothing so much as they are on the imagination and initiative of the administrator. His words and deeds must be such that the board will feel justified in granting him the freedom and decision essential to progress.

21. *The administrator will ensure a steady supply of appropriate instructional materials needed to implement his programme:* The administrator must assume total responsibility in the selection and procurement of instructional materials. The instructor, to be sure, is central to adequate instruction, but even good instructors can do better when they are provided with appropriate tools.

The first task in this area is that of budget provision. Budget-building at its best assumes that programme development has gone forward; and that the materials needed to implement such a programme will become the basis for the budget request. For instance, if it has been decided that every medical technology student should have actual experience using laboratory equipment and supplies, the budget request will be quite different from one based upon a course that is to be taught with the textbook-demonstration-lecture approach.

Even assuming this kind of budget approach, however, it will usually be the administrator who must convince the board of education and the community that expenditures for instructional materials are indispensable to an adequate programme of instruction. Sometimes elaborate plant and grounds—the outside facade of the school—win out over books, maps and other instructional aids when budgets become tight. Without deprecating adequate programmes of plant operation and

maintenance, administrators need to be able to hold the line for budget items intimately related to the instructional programme.

In the past, even though technical-vocational education has often involved extensive use of tools and similar equipment, there has been relatively little systematic use of instructional media as a means of stimulating and improving learning or of providing learning opportunities for increasing numbers of students with a wide variety of interests. Paradoxically enough, this is one branch of education where the media could be of maximum benefit. For example, it has been noted that audio tapes could be used with great advantage in machine tool shops to teach recognition and/or discrimination of relevant audio stimuli, or to present the sound of machine or tool with which students will be working, or sounds identifying malfunctions of the machine or tool to permit student discriminations among proper functions and malfunctions indicated by sounds.

Visual media is known to help promote the " discovery" or "inquiry" approach to learning and teaching. For example, 8 mm continuous loop films are frequently used for discovery teaching in technological subjects. Students keep watching the loops until they perceive the relationships represented by the visuals and then they go on to "discover" the priciples that explain these relationships. Full length 16 mm films are used effectively for teaching performance skills, facts, and for modifying certain kinds of attitudes.

Instructional media in technical-vocational education is often utilized to recreate, sometimes with remarkable accuracy, the world of work—complete with auto shop equipment, electronic assemblies, electric typewriters or whatever is required. Purchasing and updating the equipment for such courses can be rather expensive though sometimes agreements can be made with industry. If vocational education courses have to attempt to teach with outdated equipment that does not represent current realities, they lose much of their value. However, full scale materials for these courses can be supplemented by some representations, including pictures, slides, filmstrips, models and cutaways. Printed realia for these courses are relatively easy to keep current, particularly for business and distributive education. These particular courses should include local business forms and records, business handbooks and instruction manuals, reference books on business trades, and industry as well as trade newsletters, publications, periodicals, advertisements, etc. These fields also have relatively competent educational periodicals, which succeed relatively well in reviewing current materials. Other useful

instructional materials are pamphlets, posters, charts, graphs and picture. Slides—both homemade and commercial—are good teaching devices, particularly for manual skills.

The development of sophisticated instructional media and our growing knowledge of how to use these media for effective learning have opened up instructional options not only for students in formal technical-vocational institutions but also for learners outside such institutions. Today, virtually any institutional setting can become a "classroom", with the aid of and sometimes even near total dependence upon, instructional technology.

Business, industrial and financial institutions have today become major settings for instruction. No one knows exactly how much major multinational corporations spend annually on "in house" education and training of their employees (estimates range upward from $ 10 billion), but it is certain that the sum is tremendous and that it has begun to approach that spent on public education in major industrialized nations. Many labour unions operate extensive training programmes for their members, and some have even included funding for membership education in their contract negotiations.

The fact remains, however, that the effectiveness of instructional media and media technology depends ultimately on the teacher, whatever the instructional setting. It is *how* the media are used that is instructionally important, not *where* they are used.

In the actual selection of instructional materials, teachers should play a large part. It has been found that teachers feel strongly the need to assume responsibility for those activities which have to do with instruction. It behooves administrators, therefore, to devise ways by which teacher participation in instructional matters, including the selection of instructional materials, can be encouraged. It should be recognized, however, that since such participation does take time, it must be regarded as a part of the total load of the teacher.

When budget provision for instructional materials has been made and when teachers have assisted in the actual selection of materials, there still remain the problems of procurement and delivery. These are tasks which the administration of a school district should perform with the greatest possible dispatch. Nothing is as exasperating to an instructor as to participate in a budget-building or a materials-selection programme and then have purchase or delivery of materials delayed indefinitely by administrative red tape. The principal and those above him must cut through any such maze or avoid creating it.

22. *Appraisal or evaluation of instruction at regular intervals is an integral component of technical-vocational education:* The instructional programmes and teaching techniques in technical-vocational education must constantly be assessed for their effectiveness in view of rapid technological change. The administrator must make it certain that as instructional programmes are planned, plans for their evaluation should be formulated. Some industries allocate as much as one-sixth of their manpower to quality control. In education, unfortunately, evaluation has tended to be done with the left hand, if at all.

The situation is even worse in technical-vocational education. Occupational programme evaluations are seldom based on carefully collected and analysed information related to established criteria and objectives. The information is rarely presented in a way which lends itself to meaningful and effective recommendations by industry people. It is in the utilization of industry representatives for evaluation of school programmes that minimum effort and very little sophistication exists on the part of technical-vocational educators.

The present evaluative criteria used by technical-vocational educators, while requiring considerable time and effort to prepare, are singularly unimaginative, unrevealing and incapable of meaningful interpretation. Emphasis on initial employment of graduates is meaningless without knowing whether or not the graduates started at higher wages than new employees without school preparation. Information is needed concerning the extent to which school programmes meet industry's occupational and skill manpower needs; how many young people and adults seeking occupational education or training were denied such opportunity for whatever reason; the extent to which occupational education is an integral part of the total school programme; and a host of other considerations.

The solution to the problem lies in the development of evaluative criteria checklists by educators in cooperation with industry-representatives. While checklists of questions used in evaluating a programme do not necessarily mean that standards exist against which findings may be compared, it will not be too long before such standards will be forthcoming—at the national, regional and local levels. Such standards are desperately needed and might well be a "first order of business" for research by government agencies and university departments of education.

More than this, occupational programme educators and industry representatives must be concerned with the purpose of evaluation, *i.e.*,

stimulation of needed improvements and provisions for advance planning to meet anticipated needs. The travail and labour of the evaluation process and preparation of detailed reports are useless unless recommended actions for improvement are forthcoming. To help assure that evaluation reports receive attention by school authorities, the call of evaluation must originate with these officials. In the second place, it is necessary that specific programme evaluation reports be studied and consolidated into a report of the total occupational programme of the school system. This consolidated report should provide for interpretation of findings and establishment of priorities for action and should be presented in a manner meaningful to boards of education. The process of analysis, interpretation and presentation should be a cooperative effort on the school system administrators, programme supervisors and industry representatives.

To sum up then, periodic programme evaluation is a major responsibility of school administrators. They can be substantially assisted in evaluating programmes of technical-vocational education by representatives of industry, usually organized as advisory committees, both for specific occupational programmes and for the total technical-vocational programme of the school or school system. Industry representatives will involve themselves in visiting school programmes, questioning teachers, students and administrators, and becoming intimately acquainted with educational philosophy, policies and practices, for general as well as technical-vocational education, so that they may better understand the implications of the information obtained. School authorities or the boards of education must recognize that a great deal of time and effort is required for the preparation of programme evaluation reports. And in recognizing this, they should take some action, even if it is only to inform the evaluators why it is not possible to take action on the recommendations. In the event of such situations, the school administrators may be surprised at the offers of assistance they might receive from industry to implement the recommendations contained in the reports.

Whether the administrator assesses the training programmes himself or in cooperation with industry, he does it so by using the standard evaluation procedure which has the following steps:

(i) The formulation of objectives.
(ii) The definition of these objectives in behavioural terms.
(iii) Determination of places where these behaviours may be observed.

(iv) Selection or development of instruments upon which to record these behaviours when observed.
(v) Appraisal and interpretation of the evidence thus collected.

If done correctly this process is, of course, a rather laborious one. All aspects of an instructional programme probably cannot be submitted continuously to such a careful procedure. On the other hand, the spirit of the evaluative approach can be applied much more generally than is now the case. Essentially, such an approach stresses careful formulation of purposes and collection of evidence in terms of those purposes.

Administrators need to help instructional staff and lay citizens alike to see that evaluation is a necessary complement to planning and doing. If we devise a new programme for the teaching of secretarial science, we must, of course, try it out, and we must evaluate, as best we can, how effective the programme has been. Planning, doing, and evaluating are in a real sense, just parts of a whole.

23. *The administrator should follow approved business and accounting policies and practices in the management of school finance:* As head of a technical-vocational school, the principal is also a business manager. Since public schools spend public money, the school administrator shares the responsibility for seeing that the public gets its money's worth. This is not to say that he is responsible for running the institution cheaply—for *saving* money. Rather, he is responsible for *spending* wisely. He must always be able to prove that he has done this well.

Administrators must know and understand the sources of school revenue at local, provincial, and central levels. They should also help teachers and patrons to understand what these sources are. Not only do administrators need to administer honestly and efficiently the internal funds in connection with extra-class activity, but they also must be able, at all times, to prove that their administration of such funds has been honest and efficient. Although these basic principles have been emphasized in school administration courses for a generation, financial problems have grown more complex, and the need for their emphasis is greater than ever. Many administrators who have been honest in their handling of student funds have found themselves in difficulty because they were unable to prove their honesty. And they have learned by bitter experience the importance of well-kept financial records. This topic is discussed in greater detail in a separate chapter dealing with school finance.

24. *The administrator will be responsible for the overall supervision*

of school plant management programme: The establishment of an expensive institution of technical-vocational learning in a community does not guarantee that the trainees will be adequately housed or that instructors will be able to provide a sound training programme. If the facilities and equipment are not properly cared for on a daily basis or if general maintenance programmes are inadequate the educational environment of the students may be seriously handicapped.

Proper care of the school grounds and the exterior of the school buildings will be a positive factor in school-community relations and should also extend the useful life of the building, but the relative efficiency of the daily custodial and maintenance programme will have a more direct effect upon the daily operation of the educational programmes. General housekeeping practices and trouble-free performance of various pieces of equipment will have a direct effect upon teacher effectiveness.

For accounting purposes and for better understanding of duties and functions, school plant management activities are generally divided into two areas—operation and maintenance. These two terms may be defined as follows:

Operation of Plant: Activities necessary to keep the school buildings open and ready for use, including cleaning, disinfecting, moving furniture, operating telephone switchboards, making minor adjustments, and performing other housekeeping duties on a regular basis, either daily, weekly, monthly or seasonally.

Maintenance of Plant: Activities necessary to keep the grounds, facilities and equipment at their original condition of completeness and efficiency, either through repairs or by replacement of anything less than a total building.

The administrator must ensure that activities in both the areas are performed regularly and efficiently. Also, he must see that everyone connected with the school assumes appropriate responsibility in the management of the school plant; and must define clearly the responsibility that each individual has. Much of the day-to-day success of the instructional programme will depend on the services that are provided by custodial and maintenance personnel. Daily housekeeping tasks must be performed and faculty equipment and furniture must receive immediate attention if teachers are to work effectively with students. As the use of various instructional aids and equipment continues to increase, the interdependence between the quality of the custodial and maintenance programme and the level of learning efficiency will become more evident.

The general atmosphere and appearance of the institution will also affect the way in which teachers and students view their daily tasks and the personal responsibility which they assume for good housekeeping practices. Orderly, clean, and attractive surroundings create a psychological and physical environment which has a positive effect upon student and faculty performance, morale and conduct.

25. *The administrator will strive to develop a positive programme of discipline in his institution to maintain proper standards of student conduct:* A proper criterion for judging the success of the administration of any educational institution is his ability to maintain standards of student conduct appropriate to a good setting for learning; if he lacks this ability, he is in trouble. Instructors expect the administrator to be their most dependable source of assistance in dealing with difficult cases. His superiors in the chain of command and the members of the board of education expect to be informed on serious discipline problems, but for the most part they delegate to the administrator the responsibility for these matters in his school. Students recognize him as the man in charge as well as a friend and counsellor in episodes of misbehaviour on their part.

Whether he likes it or not, most people look upon him as the "disciplinarian" of the school. The administrator cannot disregard matters of discipline and is obliged to do as much as possible to develop a positive programme in his school.

At no time in the history of education have administrators so compelled to exercise discipline policies and practices as they have to do now. Many are torn between taking a firm stand and relaxing normal regulations. The effectiveness of traditional behaviour patterns of principals, teachers and students with respect to maintaining discipline has been challenged, particularly by students and their supporters. Student unrest, strikes, demonstrations, confrontation, and affiliation with undesirable political elements and militant groups have complicated the lives of all concerned. Responding to student demands has become a common experience rather than exception for school administrators.

For years discipline in educational establishments meant punishment for the violation of rules and the enforcement of regulations imposed upon students by the authorities. This concept still prevails, however, discipline is also a process of education designed to improve and perfect behaviour; furthermore, discipline may have as its goal obedience to rules based on self-control or self-discipline. Present day educators are in general agreement that, although discipline still involves the

establishment of rules and regulations, the major emphasis should be on securing a high degree of self-discipline in students.

26. *The administration of the modern technical-vocational school must assume keen interest in maintaining an efficient system of pupil personnel record:* A well-planned and carefully maintained system of pupil personnel records is essential if the administrator is going to meet the numerous requests for information about his students and his school. The purposes of the pupil personnel record system are: (i) to record the achievement and growth of a student during his school career, (ii) to provide information necessary in preparing reports required by the local board of education, the state, industry and various professional boards and associations, (iii) to report to parents on the progress of their wards, (iv) to provide information needed by teachers and counsellor in working with students, and (v) to provide information needed by higher institutions and employers about former students.

The role of the administrator is to ensure that certain guidelines are followed in building an efficient system of pupil personnel records for his institution. Some of the important guiding principles are listed below:

(i) Each record should score a clearly defined purpose.
(ii) Only information that will be used shall be included in school records.
(iii) Few demands should be made upon teachers to maintain pupil records.
(iv) All records should be as simple as will serve the purpose intended.
(v) Personal record of pupils should be readily accessible to the faculty.
(vi) Repetition of information should be reduced to a minimum.
(vii) Records should be housed so as to prevent loss and tampering.
(viii) Pupil personnel records should be revised as school practices and needs change.

27. *The administrator will lend active support to the area of non-classroom educational activities:* Non-classroom educational activities, commonly known as extra-curricular activities are a special set of programmes whose purpose is to provide the student with channels through which he can express his talents and interests within a sanctioned social environment in company with his peers. Properly planned and executed, these activities enhance and reinforce the purposes of the institution.

Capitalizing upon the strong adolescent tendency to band together for activities which are intrinsically interesting to them, the extra-curricular activities create an atmosphere of zest and relevancy within the institution.

So that the activity programme can bolster, rather than impede, the institution's basic programme objectives five guiding principles require adherence. These are:

(i) Activities should be meaningfully related to school purposes.
(ii) Activities should be built upon genuine student interest.
(iii) Activities must be controlled by the school.
(iv) Activities should be open to all.
(v) Activities should be financially supported.

Types of activities can be classified as athletic activities, student union activities, club programmes, social and assembly type activities, community-related activities and performing activities.

The administrator of the school can play an important role in administering this phase of the total educational enterprise by actively supporting, financing, staffing and supervising it.

SUMMARY

This chapter outlines strategies through which technical-vocational education may be administered effectively. A number of guiding principles and administrative methods are discussed which apply to this phase of education. Chief amongst them are:

1. The primary purpose of technical-vocational education is to prepare each student to enter and progress in socially useful employment.
2. It must be provided to young and old alike.
3. It must draw its content of study from an analysis of occupations.
4. It should be broad enough to include all factors contributing to occupational adequacy.
5. It must be flexible and dynamic.
6. Administration must be recognized as a decision-making process.
7. Administration must be based on well-defined policies.
8. Each person involved in the instruction of a vocational programme must have a clear understanding of its objectives.

9. Charts of organization and work distribution are essential for efficient administration of school programmes.
10. The administrator should have a clear understanding of the legal structure under which he operates.
11. The instructors must possess recognized competency in their area of instruction and should know basic principles of pedagogy.
12. The administrator must maintain strong links with industry which can be of tremendous help to his instructional programmes.
13. Vocational guidance must be an integral component of technical-vocational education.
14. Adequate space, time and equipment must be provided to assure quality instruction.
15. Vocational programmes should be designed for students of all ability levels.
16. Apprenticeship training programmes should be recognized as integral components of technical-vocational education and must be initiated, implemented and supervised with care.
17. Occupational programme should be developed according to the needs of the community served.
18. The training strategy must recognize the demographic changes, technological developments and economic shifts taking place in the society.
19. Good public relations programmes are crucial to the success of technical-vocational programmes.
20. The administrator must maintain proper and cordial relations with the board of education which controls the activities of his institution.
21. Appropriate instructional materials must be provided in ample and steady supply to implement effective instruction.
22. Training programmes must be evaluated at regular intervals.
23. School finance must be managed in a professional manner.
24. Proper maintenance of school property and building is necessary in order to prolong its life and to give it an aesthetic look.
25. The administrator should strive to develop a *positive* programme of student discipline in his school.
26. Pupil personnel records must be well-planned and carefully maintained.
27. Extra-curricular or non-classroom activities should be actively supported by the administrator.

4

Administrator's Perception of the Structure of Business and Industry

Administrators and supervisors in technical-vocational education are engaged not only in the task of preparing people to perform the skills and acquire the knowledge and attitude desired by society but giving them a practical understanding of the environment into which they will go. That presumes a general and continuous study of the socio-economic milieu on the part of those who direct the programme. How far the desired understanding can be developed in students will depend on many factors not the least of which is the interest such people have in gaining these understandings. Their native ability to deal with principles in the fields involved and to apply those principles to the practical concerns of working and earning also plays an important part.

It is probably true that students engaged in vocational programmes dislike, and in some cases actively resist, what they regard as abstract "book learning". Usually, they want to learn what has to be learned and to get on with the job as soon as possible. To study anything that sounds like economics, history, or literature is almost anathema to them. They have had enough of that, they often say. They came to this programme to rid themselves of it. This is a challenge to nomenclature and methodolgy. We do not have to call the subject economics. And the methodological approach, if suited to the interests and ability of these students, will help to catch and hold attention.

The desired understandings have to find a way into instructional content of the courses offered in the school or programme. The urgency becomes more obvious as the complexity of society increases. Broadly classified, the instructional material concerns economics and the structure of business and industry because economics today is at the base of the whole enterprise. We often ignore, while teaching this course, the philosophical and institutional concepts which must have their place in a

programme of liberal education. Vocational education is not on a crusade; it should not concern itself with making the world a better place to live in, badly though the world may need improving, but in preparing people to live as economically viable units in the society we have. It would be enough if vocational administrators and supervisors adhered to those practical and measurable goals for which their programmes have been organized.

We have then to consider those basic economic factors and their development to provide background and interest in continued study so that those responsible for the direction of programmes will be better able to perform their task. Hopefully, some of the emphasis will find way into the courses of study in technical and vocational schools. We have to concern ourselves then with the function of business and industry as it is; the types of organizations, employment practices, changes due to mechanization, function in training and retraining, place of unions, and the function of governments at various levels in the training and retraining of workers.

BASIC ECONOMIC FACTORS

In this field, we meet terms such as private enterprise, free enterprise, *laissez faire,* profit making, profit sharing, and many others. These terms, like so many words in the English language, mean so many things to so many different people that we must take a closer look at them. Consider "private enterprise" for example. What does it mean in practical terms? To some it describes the whole system under which personal and private initiative has free rein in a competitive milieu to operate for personal gain with a minimum of governmental interference. It operates, at least in theory, on the Jeffersonian principle that the government that governs the least is the best type of government.

But some may well ask: How private is an empire like Tata's, Birla's, General Motors, IBM or SONY, which are larger and more powerful than many governments with which they deal? A fellow operating a one-man shop comes as close as anything we have to private enterprise, but what with the requirements of various government agencies this one fellow can be heard to complain that he is not running his business any more. How free then is free enterprise under these conditions?

Laissez faire, or the "let be" concept, which is based on the free operation of the law of supply and demand in the market-place, is compromised as soon as one law is passed regulating tariffs or imposing

taxes. It is impossible to define these terms today in any manner that will satisfy the entrepreneur in his claimed right of freedom to develop his own business in his own way.

Profit making and profit sharing are terms with which all interested in technical-vocational education must be familiar. Administrators and students alike should recognize and accept the hard fact that in any modern industrialized society somebody, somewhere, has to make a profit doing something. There is no easily recognized authoritative statement from any source, capitalist or communist, that denies this. There has to be a margin between a cost and a selling price, be it rupees, dollars or rubles. Profit sharing is not new but its applications to modern industry and its rationalization are new and sometimes difficult to develop. Where it has been accomplished through the cooperative efforts of workers and management alike, it seems to have much to recommend it.

Students in modern schools must be brought to understand that business and industry exist to make a profit from the production of goods and provisions of services. This has been true since at least the beginning of organized enterprise. Human nature and its characteristics of selfish ambition necessitated government controls. These controls were perfected over years and made into binding laws. It is a continuous process. But how far the controls be allowed to go without serious damage to the system? These are matters that should have relevance to the drafters of vocational programmes.

TYPES OF ORGANIZATIONS

Business and industry have an organizational structure of their own. Authority flows from top to bottom of enterprise with advisory personnel set off-side for specialized duties as indicated by their title. On a flow chart, the full lines show the direction of authority while dotted lines are used to point up the advisory function. There are modifications of this generalization depending on a great variety of factors chiefly those having to do with the kind of industry, tradition, impact of management personality etc., but the line of authority cannot be mistaken.

It can safely be assumed that the large aggregations of labour and capital are situated in those parts of the country where industries are concentrated. Even here the greater number of people employed are in the smaller industries employing per unit relatively few people, organized strictly on line-staff principles. The further away one gets from these concentrations the preponderance of smaller industries and the total

employment become more significant to the organization of technical-vocational programmes, and to the content of teaching materials in both shops and classrooms.

The factor of impersonality varies from the small business or industry to the large. The worker in a small enterprise is in close contact with the boss and there is no social or employer-employee distinction between them. Not infrequently they are personal friends. As the business or industry grows it takes on the characteristics of corporate management. The actual ownership may come to reside in thousands upon thousands of stock holders while the control may rest in a small group whose executive officer is a trained manager who has little or no personal stake in the enterprise. The assembly line worker never sees the boss; the foreman is the management to him. It is this factor of impersonality that has caused much of the adversative nature of the relationship between employer and employee in this day.

All these considerations are indicative of the kind of information that should be a part of the training of administrators and supervisors for the following two reasons. First, while organizing the content of courses, the students should be made aware of the differences in organization they will encounter depending on the type of enterprise they choose to enter for employment, and to prepare them for conditions as they will find them. Secondly, they must be made aware of the organization of the administrative structure of the school or programme itself.

EMPLOYMENT POLICIES AND PRACTICES

Nowhere is there greater variation among census groupings than in employment policies and practices as they are related to the size of the enterprise. First, in the matter of policy—the norm is to find the best worker, either potential or trained, for the job in hand. An employer may overlook a hundred without thinking twice if he finds one who fills the particular job specification. The task of business and industry is not to make the maximum use of human resources in the interest of society as a whole but to make the maximum use of those resources to the benefit of the particular business or industry.

Put rather bluntly, it is the employer's business to select people who will produce the goods in the most economical manner, at a maximum profit. He does not consider it his responsibility to advise people in selecting their occupations. That he leaves to some private agencies, to

schools, to welfare departments and the like. It may sound rather callous but this is how the business world operates.

The size of the organization helps shape its practices. The operator of a small automobile repair shop employing himself and two mechanics needs a replacement for one of the employees. He contacts the local employment exchange for help. The man arrives, salary terms are discussed and the new employee goes to work. Compare this with what happens in a large industry or organization such as in the fields of oil, chemicals, insurance, automobile or many others. The prospective employee shows up at the employment office, possibly in response to an advertisement. He is put through an elaborate programme of information gathering including biographical data, medical history, etc. filling forms of various kinds. Tests of ability and aptitude are administered which are usually designed by a clinical psychologist employed by the firm itself. It is the function of the administrator to ensure that the students are prepared to meet these conditions.

The public service presents a minor variation from the employment practices discussed above. It is concerned with getting people who have the knowledge and skill to do a particular kind of work. The variation, however, occurs in that if a person seeks employment, the personnel officer will try to find a place in the organization where the applicant can be employed to the best advantage to the organization and to himself.

Most large organizations have recently developed programmes for the upgrading of their personnel. Apart from the special skills needed for particular jobs, such organizations ensure that their employees have acquired knowledge of how to conduct themselves in the organization in such matters as insurance, accidents, health benefits, promotions etc. When jobs change these employers consider it worthwhile to save that stored knowledge in their own interest. So, opportunities are offered for employees to upgrade themselves rather than for the employer to take on new workers who do not know their way around in the organization.

Provincial or federal agengies sometimes cooperate in these efforts by private industry, especially in supervisory training. But it is not only in the area of supervisor training that attempts are made to improve the relationships between supervisor and supervised, but upgrading in the knowledge and skills of a highly technical content is available today in many firms as the demand for skilled manpower becomes acute.

Thus, it seems that in the interest of self-preservation, many industries are adapting their employment practices to the improvements made in the selection, training and maintenance of staff. They are doing it within the

established policy of sustaining profits within a competitive societal structure. Here again there is the importance to supervisors and administrators of familiarizing themselves with the conditions relative to employment locally and across the entire spectrum of business and industry. Courses must be set to give students clear understanding of the environment into which they will go and know how to deal with it through the learning acquired in the institutional programme.

ECONOMIC AND SOCIAL CHANGES

A separate chapter deals with trends affecting programmes of vocational education in which extrapolation of current changes in the socio-economic scene are discussed. Here, only a brief statement shall be made of some of the shifts regarded as significant to those who administer and supervise vocational programmes. In some cases, the administrators would be doing something to make programmes responsive to those changes and in others, to maintain merely a strict watch. It cannot be too often said that administrators in technical-vocational education should, at all times, be sensitive to variations in the social and economic environment into which their students will be going. Many changes that can be classified as economic have taken place during the previous half century. Here we discuss two in detail: changing patterns of business financing, and automation.

The financing of business and industry now is significantly different from what it was a few years ago, although the changes here were not as radical as have taken place in the area of consumer financing. Before the depression of the 1930s people generally expected that there would be recurring cycles of business boom and bust. So general was this expectation that preparations were made for a recession after World War II. Not only the large corporations but the governments had actually planned for it. Nothing of that nature happened. Western economies boomed until the mid-fifties when a slight recession occurred. The reasons for this make a very interesting study.

Probably the major causative factor was that governments had learned of the manipulation of credit through control of bank rates, long and short-term financing, rescheduling of loans, etc. The net result is that industry, businesses and governments now allow for inflation before making any estimations of any increases in their annual budget. For most industrialized countries of the west, it is about 8 per cent per year.

The second change—automation—is of great importance to those

who supervise technical-vocational education programmes. Automation to some people is almost indistinguishable from mechanization, whereas by others it is held to a more precise meaning to describe processes controlled by electronic devices in whole or in part. For example, the rotating bobbin in sewing machines was an improvement over the reciprocating bobbin, which not only extended the life of the machine but produced more and better work, especially with high speed machines. That was merely technological change caused by an improved machine with no change in power control. Of quite a different order is a loom in a textile plant, entirely encased, turning out ten times more cloth than the old one. Not only that, in terms of manpower, the new loom has only one man, replacing eight of the past, whose job is merely to keep watch. At the same time, the quality of the cloth is much better compared to the one in the past. If anything goes wrong, anywhere in the process, the machine automatically stops and a red light flashes to indicate where the trouble is. All this is controlled by electronic devices. This is true automation which is being an integral component of nearly all modern industry in the West.

Automation has not fully arrived in the third world yet and its impact is still of a minimal nature. The reasons for this limited impact are mainly costs, and the size of the operation which indicates the amount of work to be done. The utilization factor is important because such equipment cannot be allowed to lie idle. It must justify its cost in use.

How is automation going to affect the technician of the future? Is it going to replace him in the workshop, laboratory, or the plant? A pessimistic concern has been expressed by some who maintain that service activities will also tend to displace workers by becoming self-service, by becoming cybernated, and by being eliminated. Others, however, are optimistic about automation. They think that science fiction writers have created a false picture of automation as an uncontrolled giant. These people hold that we must remove automation technology from the realm of science fiction and reveal it for what it really is—nothing more than down-to-earth continuation of our basic manufacturing tools and methods.

To meet the future challenges of automation we shall have to make some changes in our present educational programme. As administrators, it should be our prime aim to support continuing education as the primary response to the challenges of automation and technological change. In our dynamic society the acceleration and accumulation of knowledge is proceeding in geometrical progression. To keep up with such rapid change

in technology, the graduates of vocational education programmes would require refresher or extension courses at regular intervals. No matter how willing the new graduate may be in trying to keep up with the changes in his field, on a personal basis, he will have the need of systematic organized educational experience to assist him. Administrators and supervisors of vocational education will have to think in terms of revising the curriculum, along with the whole scheme of work, to make possible a life-time education.

Another change in existing educational programme which is needed to cope with the challenge of automation in the future is a greater emphasis upon principles, rather than techniques. Greater stress should be put upon a deeper understanding of basic technical concepts rather than the methodology, for even an exhaustive training cannot cover all the known and needed techniques in detail. In addition, mere procedures increasingly become obsolete before they can be taught, much less applied.

We now turn to the social aspects of the current scene which administrators should not ignore even though they may emphasize the economic phases and influences. Social and occupational patterns are shifting so that increasing number of people now nearing thirty years of age have never worked but have been supported by their families since they became of working age. This is most evident in the larger centres of population where these shifts have been most seriously felt. Idleness and the effects on personality of the lack of socially useful and significant work shows up on some cases in strikes, violence, crimes and drug addiction, which some youthful offenders attribute to sheer boredom.

The proportion of white collar jobs in relation to all others is increasing for both men and women. They are being forced into different kinds of jobs than those traditionally accepted. Women are being encouraged to enter the technical and engineering fields.

The effects of these changes on the objectives of education are of social as well as occupational significance. If people are going to do less and less for more and more, does it not naturally follow that the worthy and satisfactory use of leisure becomes more important as an educational goal? Every authoritative statement of educational objectives has included this among its pronouncements. The social effects of these occupational patterns are too complicated even to assess without the most careful research but there ought to be an awareness of them. Composite schools in the United States and in the United Kingdom are stressing education for leisure.

There is another effect on education from these changes that has

already come about: vocational training for flexibility or adaptability. In most vocational programmes the idea is to give basic training in the mechanical processes characteristic of certain types of industry and leave it to the industries to give the specialized training. Usually such programmes end up as failures. The reason for the failure is mainly that when trainees go out to get jobs they are confronted with the demand for people who could perform specialized skills. One can ascertain this fact by scanning the employment advertisements in any newspaper.

An attempt by educators to meet the problem was to train people in the specialities that are in demand and encourage them, when the jobs become obsolete, to return to the vocational programmes for retraining. It has been stated with good evidence that the speed with which changes are taking place today make it necessary for a worker to change trades or occupations several times during the span of their work life.

THE FUNCTION OF BUSINESS AND INDUSTRY IN TRAINING AND RETRAINING

We must keep in mind at all times that the primary purpose of business and industry is the production of goods and services as a means of profit earning. Self-preservation, under certain conditions, dictates assumption of the training function by private agencies in both fields: manufacturing and distribution. The degree to which business and industry assume this function varies. It is totally at private expense in some places; in others the costs and responsibilities are shared with other agencies which may be organized labour or may be government at some or all levels; in still others both the training and retraining functions are assumed by governments.

Some industries have good reasons for preferring to do their own training as is the situation in Switzerland and West Germany. Many industries in those countries find it easier to provide the necessary flexibility, specialization adapted to plant needs, easy transition from training to production and other advantages. Other industries, such as those characterized by heavy machinery, do not lend themselves to institutional training regardless of location.

Industry does have a function to perform in both training and retraining because tax supported programmes could not do the entire job even if society wanted them to. It is probably true that publicity supported programmes in the developing world could do much more than they are now doing to the advantage of both society and industry.

The main areas where business and industry will continue to do all their own skill training are paper and pulp mills, oil and chemical industries, and heavy equipment industries. Plants here are too costly and utilization of equipment for training cannot be spared from production. It is to be noted that these factors do not apply to the engineering and technical fields as they do to training at the secondary level.

An area where industry and tax-supported programme together can operate effectively is in the apprenticeship and cooperative education schemes where industry and business do what they can best do and the same applies to organized labour and to governments. Problems arise at the points where the programmes have to be integrated, but given the desired attitudes on the parts of all concerned, these problems are easily sorted out.

The issue of re-training has come into prominence because of mechanization of industry and its modern development, automation. The current cry for adaptability and flexibility, and the attempts by education to deal with it have been previously mentioned. There is some doubt whether much can be done to educate for change, but certainly well-organized sequences designed to retrain workers in special skills in immediate demand can be useful. The very speed with which changes come about today make this the most promising approach.

THE PLACE OF UNIONS

Organized labour has a part to play in the overall plan of technical-vocational education and training. The early struggles of workers to establish corporate efforts in their own behalf are well known to anyone familiar with the record of the rise of industrialization. The conditions under which workers laboured and lived in the earliest days of the factories in England make sorry reading. The *laissez faire* economics of the 18th century left little chance for the voices of children to be heard from the mines and factories and any attempt to alter conditions for the better met with bitter resistance from the entrepreneurs.

The first struggles of the workers were for the right to organize, followed by demands for better working conditions and wages that would permit living in respect to their status as human beings. That struggle still goes on in some parts of the world but in the advanced industrialized countries a stage has now been reached where many leaders of organized labour are as well educated as the captains of industry with whom they have to deal. Also, the members of most unions have acquired a

sophistication that permits the advancement of their interests in accordance with the good of society as a whole.

Much remains to be done along these lines as some statutes governing the activities of organized labour indicate, because with the power unions have acquired has come abuses of that power employed to the detriment of the public interest. Any authoritative history of the last 200 years must show that unions are almost entirely responsible for the improvement of working conditions and pay, and the gains have been won against the determined opposition of entrenched management. Hopefully, it now appears that management and labour are learning to live together and with the financial resources and the organized power of many of the unions, the assigning of the analogy of the lamb to labour and the lion to management is no longer applicable.

The philosophy of unionism is still generally adversative. It operates with some exception to this in a few countries, chiefly in Scandinavia. In Sweden, specifically, strikes have been avoided for years. This rivalary is based on the idea that the worker and managers are adversaries; that the interests of management and labour are antithetical, that they must do constant battle to reach a state of compromise, satisfactory to both sides. There are some flaws in this position which are beginning to be realized by both contending parties.

In recent years, lines of cooperation in the developmental process are beginning to show. The establishment of voluntarily cooperating representative groups with mediatory and consultative machinery are being set up supported by legislation through which labour and management work as a team. A new type of union leader is emerging—informed in history and economics, trained in parliamentary procedures, sensitive to human relations aspects, and conscious of the part unions can play in the preparation of future generation of workers.

It becomes clear that organized labour has an important part to play in training and re-training. Labour's representatives sit on boards and councils at all levels—from the National Advisory Council to the Advisory committees in the small trade or vocational school. But it is not only in an advisory capacity that labour serves but also through the cooperation of individual members on the shop floors, in their attitudes towards new workers.

Unions have an even more definite function to perform in the field of apprenticeship where the attitudes of workers mentioned earlier often hampered the learning process for some young workers. There is a new acceptance of the social responsibility that unions must ensure a steady

supply of skilled manpower to the society. The move to have apprentices indentured to unions points in this direction. This is especially true where industries are small and their permanence questionable.

One area where unions can be helpful is in informing its members about the need for re-training and making them aware of accelerating change under the impact of modern conditions. Governments, management and labour, working as a team can do much to face new realities created by these changes. It is natural for the older workers to resist change and to refuse learning new skills as those they have practiced for years become obsolete. But their fellow workers and union leaders can do much to prepare them for such inevitable necessities.

SUMMARY

This chapter describes the milieu, economic and social, within which administrators and supervisors have to work. The materials presented here are indicative of the direction in which technical-vocational education must go in order to render the maximum service to society. There is also a review of some basic economic factors and recent changes occurring in trade and industry. Employment policies and practices are discussed with the variations in them dependent on such elements as size and location of business.

It is emphasized that change is not new but the speed of occupational shift in response to such innovations as automation is new. This fact must be understood by the administrators and the programmes under their direction must respond. The two most significant changes are trade and financing patterns and automation. The most obvious effects of automation are pointed out. The changes in the social lives of people as the resultant of occupational shifts are many, but an important one to vocational educators is the current emphasis on the wise use of leisure.

The problem of re-training is dealt with in relation to the current emphasis on education for adaptability and flexibility necessitated by changing occupational patterns. Lastly, the role played by the labour unions in business and industry is discussed along with its implications to the administrators of technical-vocational education.

5

Leadership Dimensions of Administration

A primary function of the administrator is to provide leadership. For the most part, unfortunately, the administrators are neither coping nor leading. One reason is that many of us in the educational set up misconceive what leadership is all about. *Leading* does not mean *managing*: the difference between the two is crucial. Most of us are acquainted with many institutions that are very well *managed* and very poorly *led*. They may excel in the ability to handle daily routines and yet never ask whether the particular routine should exist at all. To lead, so the dictionary tells us, is to go in advance of, to show the way, to influence or induce, to guide in direction, course, action, opinion. To manage means to bring about, to accomplish, to have charge of or responsibility for, to conduct. The difference may be summarized as activities of vision and judgment *versus* activities of efficiency.

In his decision-making, the leader today has to deal with four groups or agencies—his immediate management team, constituencies within his organization, forces outside his organization and the media. While his decisions and actions affect the people of these four groups, their decisions and actions, too, affect him.

LEADERSHIP QUALITIES

Leadership has nothing to do with status. Most leaders are unrecognized until something goes wrong and brings about these special qualities—knowledge, courage, decisiveness, dependability, initiative, tact, justice, enthusiasm and humour, judgment and common sense, tenacity and self-control. Perhaps the supreme quality in a leader is confidence. As we know, proper administration is essentially a question of the organization of manpower, materials, resources, and strategy for the accomplishment of a desired goal. This is impossible unless the administrator has enough

self-confidence and is so well organized as to intelligently understand the causes of the problems encountered in day-to-day work and the remedies for their adequate solution. It requires therefore an intimate knowledge and understanding of a great many factors, including people as well as materials, plus a great deal of curiosity, imagination, determination, integrative ability and good judgment.

PRESCRIPTION FOR LEADERSHIP

At this point some of us must be shaking their heads and thinking that one must be a superman to have all the qualities listed above. It is not necessarily so and we must not think in those terms. It is an established fact that the art of leadership can be learned, it is not inborn as a natural gift. Even if we are not endowed with all the favourable leadership traits we certainly could become effective leaders as long as we recognise the following:

1. Leaders must develop the vision and strength to call the shots. There are risks in taking the initiative—but the greater risk is to wait for orders. We need leaders at every level who can lead, not just manage. This means that institutions have to realize that they need leadership, that their need is for vision, energy, and drive rather than blandness and safety.
2. The leader must be a conceptualist. A conceptualist is more than an "idea man"; he must have an entrepreneurial vision, a sense of perspective, the time and the inclination to think about the forces and raise the basic questions that will affect the destiny of both the institution and the society within which it is embedded.
3. He must have a sense of continuity and significance in order to see the present in the past and the future in the present. He must, in the compelling moments of the present, be able to clarify problems—elevate them into understandable choices for the constituents—rather than exploit them; to define issues, not aggravate them. Thus, a leader will get at the underlying issues and present a clear alternative rather than leaving the problem as a problem (for example "student indiscipline" or "incompetent teachers") or allowing the problem to stay out of control until it becomes a "crisis".
4. Leaders must learn to be bold and courageous. If a leader has

the vision, takes the time, and makes the effort to lead the way by presenting a perspective, an alternative, a choice, he will need courage. He must be allowed to take risks, to embrace error, to use his creativity fully and encourage others to do the same.

5. The leader must get at the truth and learn how to filter the unwieldy flow of information into coherent patterns. He must prevent the distortion of that information by overeager sycophants who will tailor it to satisfy what they consider to be his prejudices or vanities. The biggest problem of a leader—any leader—is getting at the truth. The politics of bureaucracy tends to interfere with rather than facilitate truth gathering.

   That's mainly true because the huge size of our educational organizations and the enormous overload burdening every leader make it impossible for him to verify all his own information, analyze all his own problems, or always decide who should or should not have his ear or time. Since he must rely for much of this upon his key assistants, he would not feel comfortable in so close and vital a relationship with people who were not at least of similar minds and compatible personalities.

   Of course, this is perfectly human and, upto a point, understandable. But the consequences can be devastating because the leader is likely to see only that highly selective information or those carefully screened people that his key assistants decide he should see. And he may discover too late that he acted on information that was inadequate or inaccurate, or that he has been shielded from "troublesome" visitors who wanted to tell him what he should have known, or that he has been protected from some problem that should have been his primary concern.

6. Lastly, to lead others, the leader must first know himself. His ultimate test is the wise use of power. He must learn to listen to himself. Also, he must learn how to listen to understand, not to evaluate. He must learn to play, to live with ambiguity and inconsistency. Most of all, the test of any leader is whether he can ride and direct the process of change and, in the process, build new strengths.

It is, therefore, clear that the administrator with the leadership qualities listed above must be three things: a trouble shooter constantly expecting

the unexpected and always ready to deal with crises, a promoter of new programmes to increase the usefulness and effectiveness of the institution, and a supervisor delegating as much as practical to subordinates.

DELEGATION

An institution functions most effectively when a capable administrator, rather than attempting to control and supervise intimately each of the various activities that make up the total programme, is able to delegate control and supervision to responsible subordinates. Second perhaps to recruitment of the best possible personnel, this is probably the most important single factor in successful administrative practice.

The administrator has to decide which responsibilities and authorities to entrust to others and which to retain. Subordinates should be allowed a role in selecting those who will report to them, or responsibility cannot be insisted upon. Subordinate executives, in turn, delegate to those next in rank such parts of their own specified responsibilities as they may choose, and so on down the line. Thus, a school principal in effect says to his department heads, "You know our instructional objectives. You know best the instructional strategy. You know the school policy. Now the job is to see that this part of the work is done. I am holding you responsible for it. It is up to you to get results."

This type of leadership pays dividends since it gives competent individuals pride in their work and encourages initiative, self-confidence, and ability. The opposite and usually unsuccessful approach is that of administrators who insist that all actions and decisions originate with them and that everything go in or out over their desks. Studies show that supervisors who gave the greatest amount of instruction and direction tend to achieve the poorest record. This approach causes department heads either to leave the institution for more reasonable and stimulating fields or to lose interest and initiative, thereby becoming intimidated "yes people" of little value to the organization. The latter, although they may appear to be obedient, gravitate into a sullen rut, secretly delighting in the event of administrative errors. Equally inevitable in such cases is the puzzlement of the administrator over the apparent lack of cooperation, understanding, and support from subordinates.

It is not to be inferred that the job of the administrator is merely to find capable subordinates, to delegate authority to them, and then to sit back in ease and watch the wheels go round. The real test of sound

leadership involves the ability, after delegating authority, to step in unobtrusively at appropriate times to give suggestions or directions on the basis of greater knowledge and a more competent understanding of overall strategy.

Delegation has been referred to as fundamentally necessary for successful administration to any organization. In fact, administration might, with considerable truth, be defined as getting things done through others. In present day large educational establishments, it is impossible for one person to do the whole job. The principal or the head of the institution should not try to handle all of the details personally; it is a physical and mental impossibility and it is not expected.

Failure to delegate has many undesirable consequences. First, and probably of least importance, is that the administrator invites a personal physical or mental breakdown, following never-ceasing, high pressure workdays coping with annoying details and sleepless nights fed by bulging briefcases. Inevitably, the organization suffers because the administrator becomes the chief bottleneck and the work is incompletely and inefficiently done. The agency loses the benefit of whatever abilities exist in the rest of the personnel, capable potential employees shy away from the uninspiring environment, and those within the organization soon ask themselves either, "Why stay?" or "What's the use of working or trying?"

Successful and effective delegation, therefore, requires a few simple considerations. The first, as noted, is that the executive must truly and consciously wants to do it. It is never a subconscious decision or action. The administrator's function is essentially that of a coordinator and stimulator of the activities of many others, each of whom has been entrusted with specific responsibilities and authorities. The position is akin to that of the conductor of a musical orchestra through whose coordinating activity melodious and inspiring music results where there might otherwise be simply noise.

Before concluding this section, it must be emphasized that delegation is in effect a loan that is never permanent and that it can be recalled at any time. Delegation is most effective in an atmosphere of mutual understanding and respect. The executive has the right to expect that the trust will not be abused or taken for granted.

LEADER'S INFLUENCE ON MORALE AND DISCIPLINE

In every institution some rules or regulations will be necessary, but if

they are to be effective, they must be few, simple, readily understood, and applicable to all. Items that may be effectively included are limited largely to such matters as the hours of work, competency in teaching, the length of the lunch period, the handling of certain records and correspondence, and holidays and leaves. The administrator's real difficulties begin at the point where objective inflexibility ends. No one can constantly police the work and behaviour of all subordinates, and even if this were possible, it would preclude the possibility of good leadership. The best to hope for, and probably most desirable in the long run, is to develop as much as possible an almost subconscious self-discipline within the group itself so that improper behaviour of a particular employee is considered by fellow employees as an infraction against their self-developed and self-enforced code of working ethics.

The administrator should always bear in mind that although most people are willing to be subordinate to good leadership, they are not willing to be subservient. Even though the person in authority may have the legal or financial power to demand obedience, the subordinate similarly has the power to refuse to obey or, what is more practical, the power to circumvent orders while appearing to obey.

In terms of what has been said, therefore, the goal for which the good administrator will aim is a cooperative team, which is probably most successfully achieved by the development of a logical organizational structure with well defined and understood lines of authority and responsibility and a well-established tradition of good self-discipline. Good personnel management depends partly on sound organization and partly on sound individual guidance, correction, reward and punishment. It has been said that the administrator must understand people and be a leader. There are two kinds of leadership, the first demonstrated by a person with superior ability whom people gladly follow and the second consisting of mere possession of authority. Authority in itself is of limited value.

The actual approach to a disciplinary action should never be casual or momentary. A series of steps should be taken. The administrator should first look inward to discover and eliminate personal bias and to discover any personal responsibility for the situation. A many-sided approach to the problem should be made; it should be looked at through the eyes of the employee, the employee's family, fellow employees and the immediate supervisor. The entire situation should be investigated, with consideration given to the condition of work at the time, the employee's past record, the morale and behaviour of the employees as a

group, the type and degree of infraction, the organization's tradition in such cases, and any outside conditions that may have influenced the employee. An attempt should be made to discover whether the failure was due to misunderstanding, an emotional upset, lack of experience, some irregularity in working conditions, poor leadership or low morale.

In a healthy institution the staff possesses a high morale which relegates discipline of any type to a position of secondary importance. For most persons the attitude and morale of the group are a sufficient guide to conduct; and where effective leadership and good supervision exist, problems of discipline largely disappear.

Poor leadership is shown by low morale of the staff—resignations, accidents, sickness, grievances and complaints, as well as slap-dash work. Morale is related to job satisfaction. Yet the effectiveness of an administrator in planning, organizing, staffing, directing, and controlling has an important consequence on the behaviour of the staff. As discussed earlier, organizing involves two aspects: the assembly of resources, and the delegation of authority and responsibility. The wise leader will never try to perform the function of subordinates, but a working administrator will always have more power over them than a non-working one. Success is shown by high morale.

PUBLIC RELATIONS DIMENSIONS OF LEADERSHIP

Technical-vocational education is a commodity that needs to be sold in the modern day, academically-oriented society. It therefore needs energetic and zealous proponents or "salesmen", in the garb of educational leaders, to make it popular. This salesmanship requires all the leadership traits that have been discussed above, and many more as the administrator has to deal with people in business and industry, parents, students, and policy-makers in addition to his regular staff. The job requires convincing the parents and the general public that technical-vocational education is an equally attractive alternative for the careers of their children. Considerable acumen in public relations is necessary to do this effectively.

There is another reason for the public relations needs of an institution of technical-vocational learning. This type of institution is usually a tax-supported public agency that belongs to the people it serves. Its existence in a democracy depends in the final analysis on their wish to maintain it. In the long run this wish can be sustained only by public understanding and satisfaction. Such reactions naturally give rise to

pride of ownership, which in turn enhances cooperation and support. Modern thinking in educational endeavours is to do things with people, not for them or to them. *With* is an important word, which when applied jointly to a health agency and the people it serves, implies everything that contributes to good public relations.

Fundamental to a successful programme of public relations should be desire to sell the *purpose* of the programme rather than to sell an institution, much less an individual. It is true that the public is interested in personalities and figureheads, but it soon tires or becomes suspicious of too frequent references to a particular individual whether it is the guidance counsellor, public relations officer, or the principal of the institution. Perhaps the most important public relations consideration for the administrator is not to regard the educational programme as a one-person show but to share credit as well as responsibility. When this policy is followed, everyone benefits, including the public.

This is not meant to imply that the school principal does not have a most important role in the public relations programme of the institution. After all, this person is responsible for leadership and for the assurance that desirable relationships are formed and maintained. Contacts must be made with other governmental officials, prominent citizens, and various important key people including representatives of the communications field in the interests of the programme for which the principal is responsible.

General Guidelines—Here are some useful public relations guidelines that you can follow to reach the public:

1. Establish contact with all news media in your community. Try to cultivate a personal relationship with representatives of business or industrial organizations who may be of some use for the future placement of the graduates of your school. Within limits of school policy and ethical conduct, be frank and direct in sharing and obtaining information. Provide information on all worthwhile activities to them, either informally or by formal release, depending on the situation. Whenever appropriate, emphasize the technical requirements of the job at hand and the professional competence of the staff to perform it.
2. Create, and be alert, to opportunities to interpret, publicize, or promote the school's programme and its importance to the community. Use such well-known devices as speaking to community groups, spot radio and television announcements, discussion programmes, and newspaper articles, as well as

whatever innovative approaches can be developed.

3. Train all members of the staff to be ambassadors of the institution. Be sure that they understand the institution's objectives, procedures, programmes and significance. Help them to develop the right attitudes and the skills to communicate. Emphasize that to many people in the community *they are the institution*, even if they are only a voice on the telephone. Help them to understand that they are regarded in this light even in their private contacts.
4. Establish Advisory committees on school's general programme and special subjects. Give these groups an opportunity to express their views frankly, not merely to react to your proposals. You need to be as interested in what they feed back to you as in what you convey to them. Remember that development of understanding involves a two-way relationship.
5. Participate in the work of community organizations. Be of assistance to other institutions whenever possible. They will increase their understanding and respect for your institution as you work with and assist them.
6. Maintain a sensitive ear to community opinion and reaction to your institution's programmes and goals. Recognize these attitudes in formulating plans.
7. Remember that a job sincerely, effectively, and courteously done is the best public relations approach of all.

SUMMARY

An efficient administrator, by necessity, has to be the leader of his flock. He/she must display the usual leadership qualities such as initiative, courage, decisiveness, dependability, justice, enthusiasm, tact, etc. in order to become a good administrator. The art of leadership can be learned, it is not inborn as a natural gift in all cases. Some of the ways by which this could be done are discussed in the chapter.

The key to good leadership and efficient administration is delegation. However, there should be no delegation without responsibility and no responsibility without representation. Unfortunately, many administrators do not adequately understand the basic principles involved in delegation. Such people become slaves to non-administrative trivia, which could easily be handled by others. Meanwhile, competent subordinates stand by helplessly, losing interest and initiative, and

becoming mere "yes men" in the process.

Poor leadership often results in problems related to discipline. Although avoidance of conditions requiring discipline is much better than successful discipline, failure to discipline when it is indicated is demoralizing to the group. Leadership ensures good morale. Poor morale is often due to not taking action at appropriate time, insincerity, biased behaviour, and failure to acknowledge superior work.

Finally, a good leader never underestimates the importance of sound public relations in order to win the understanding and cooperation of the members of the community in which his/her institution operates.

6

Planning Dimensions of Administration

Planning, a widely used term, is perhaps as widely misunderstood and misused—especially in educational affairs. Therefore, this chapter will discuss what planning is, why and where it occurs, by whom and how it is done, and how it could be used in education.

WHAT IS PLANNING?

The word planning has many meanings. Currently, it is often used as a synonym for public decision-making. It is true that many public agencies are engaged in planning, but not all decision makers—public or private—actually plan. Planning, in effect, is making current decisions in the light of their future effects and will be used in this sense throughout this chapter.

WHAT IS EDUCATIONAL PLANNING?

Educational planning is a process to produce valid information in the form of alternative courses of action, together with predicated consequences of such alternatives, to aid decision-making by those engaged in educational policy formulation and administration. The process should be capable of providing information relative to any educational problem input and should incorporate self renewal and updating as essential features.

Since the primary purpose of educational planning is to design educational policy, studies in this area include such diverse topics as curriculum selection, design of physical facilities, resource allocation strategies, cost accounting, salary schedule analysis and student population projections. The application described here illustrates how the various approaches to planning can be used to identify in one general scheme any member of these related educational planning problems.

WHY SHOULD WE PLAN?

One of the main problems of non-planners is that their actions are responses to crises. Because they must react to whatever situation they face at the moment, rather than act on the basis of anticipation, they cannot influence that situation to achieve their goals. They are like a military commander who either can force an opponent to enter battle under circumstances favourable to himself or can simply wait until forced to fight at a time and place convenient to the enemy.

Since planners are in a contest with external forces, such as competing organizations or the ever-changing social, economic, political, or technological aspects of their environment, they have two choices. Either they can pursue, over the long run, a carefully devised course of action, or they can wait until they must take action and are forced to respond in circumstances which may or may not be favourable, using whatever resources are available. Clearly, the chances of success are far greater with the first alternative.

WHERE DOES PLANNING TAKE PLACE?

To some degree, planning occurs at all levels of human organization, from the individual to the national government. For purposes of this chapter, a department in an institution or agency is considered the lowest planning entity. The next level would be the institution or agency, then a region or community that is part of a state, which in turn is part of the nation.

The major type of planning used by each level of organization varies widely within each level. The first type is project planning, which deals with operational matters of a rather narrow scope, based on problem-solving techniques and striving for efficiency. Project planning occurs at all of the aforementioned levels, but it is predominant at the department level and is only a small portion of the national planning effort.

The next type, systems planning, deals with longer range or strategic matters. It stresses the use of optimizing techniques to produce satisfactory trade-offs among a system's components, with the ultimate goal being effectiveness rather than simple efficiency. The systems plan can integrate many project plans and ensure that the allocation of resources among them is for the benefit of the total system or community, rather than for a limited segment served by some specific project. Although systems planning is possible at all levels, it would not be truly meaningful at the departmental level. Such planning could be appropriate

in large institutions or agencies that have multiple purposes or serve several clientele groups, but generally, it is used at the community level and above.

The third type is policy planning, which stresses changing value systems to achieve such objectives as equity and equality. This kind of planning establishes the overall context within which systems planning will take place. In particular, it helps produce criteria for measuring a system's effectiveness.

Policy planning is most effective at levels where mechanisms exist for developing and implementing the normative choices of our society, that is, at the level of legislative action. Normative judgments, however, also can be developed and implemented within institutions and agencies, although, in most cases, their mechanisms would be less formal.

WHO PLANS?

The preceding section has answered this question in part. It is worth noting, however, that planners at the various levels often serve in very different roles. For example, at the departmental level, they might be engaged primarily in teaching or administrative functions, with planning only an adjunct activity. Planning becomes more an administrative function at the institutional or agency level and, in some cases, the primary mission of one or more staff persons.

At the regional or community level, many agencies have staff members who engage in planning—often with support, advice, or direction from a board or committee that represents either the special interest groups affected or the entire community. Within government, professional planning staff can be found at local, state, and central levels. Once again, these people usually function with some type of board or committee, often under the direction and oversight of a legislative branch of government.

HOW PLANNING OCCURS?

The specifics of how to plan occur within a general framework or model which describes the sequence of steps in planning. Decision-making can proceed through disjointed incrementalism or through a rational approach. Basically, the first approach implies rather cautious movements in the general direction that seems advisable, the theory being that great leaps

forward, based on a rational analysis of current and predicted situations can be dangerous, because decision makers cannot really know and understand these situations and their ramifications. Thus, they might make serious mistakes because of ignorance or misinformation.

Despite its virtue of safety, incrementalism is simply too slow to respond to the rapid and urgent changes in today's world. Admittedly, the weaknesses of the rational model are all too real. Nevertheless, they are not as severe as the proponents of incrementalism assert. The rational model can be approximated, despite a lack of perfect information, using various devices, such as simulation and decision theory, to cope with uncertainties and the lack of absolutely accurate data.

Use of the rational model as a basis for planning proceeds according to the following steps:

1. Identify the desired state (*i.e.*, set goals and objectives).
2. Determine the discrepancy between the desired state and conditions that might occur if no action was taken (this involves forecasting).
3. Identify the resources that will probably be available to effect changes toward the desired state.
4. Develop feasible alternative methods for using those resources to make the necessary changes.
5. Evaluate those alternatives and select the one that seems most likely to achieve the desired results at a reasonable cost.
6. Implement the chosen alternative.
7. Appraise the performance of this alternative, then make the necessary adjustments to bring it closer to achieving the desired objectives.

Clearly, these steps are a highly simplified model of the planning process. Planning is not, and cannot be a straight forward, sequential process. Instead, it must be regarded as a cybernetic system with many iterative loops; that is, at each step along the way, the planners must be prepared to review what has occurred in all the preceding steps and to re-evaluate those activities in the light of current developments. For example, it is entirely possible that, in the process of identifying available resources (step three), the planners might discover that their initial objectives are either too high or too low. Should this occur, they must then go back and make the necessary adjustments to step one and proceed again through

step two to step three. This iterative process should be borne in mind in all considerations of planning.

THE SYSTEMS APPROACH TO PLANNING

An educational system is an example of a system designed by man for fulfilling a human purpose and subject to human control, and consisting of a combination of human and material resources. Like other social systems, it permits freedom of choice between alternative courses of action that, by modifying its structure and functions, change its operation so that its output approximates more closely to the predetermined objectives.

The systems approach is essentially comprehensive in character. The various components of the educational service are not studied in isolation but as interacting elements of the service as a whole. Thus, the physical resources, premises, equipment, teaching personnel, community needs, and educational achievements are not considered individually, but in their interactions with one another. The systems approach is also concerned with the objectives of education, and with the total situation in which physical resources, manpower and skills, influence and may be influenced by the achievement of such objectives or goals. Finally, it takes account of the fact that the educational system in its entirety is both influenced by, and influences, a variety of external forces and circumstances.

"Systems analysis" refers to any formal analysis whose purpose is to suggest a course of action by systematically examining the objectives, costs, effectiveness, and risks of alternative policies or strategies—and designing additional ones if those examined are found wanting. It is an approach to, or way of looking at, complex problems of choice under uncertainty; it is not yet a method. The broad purposes of the systems approach are the following:

1. To formulate complex problems by providing objective data and increasing the objective element in decision-making;
2. To indicate the probable consequences of alternative courses of action;
3. To inform debates on values, objectives, and allocation of resources whose purpose is to find ways of improving

performance, reducing costs or economizing in the use of manpower or resources;

4. To compare results achieved with objectives specified;
5. Generally, to assist the decision-making process in planning and management, *i.e.*, in making adjustments to the components, structure, apparatus for information and communications, and decision-making procedures of an existing organization, in order to improve its performance.

What is to be treated as a system will depend on practical considerations. For some purposes, activities carried out or educational devices are regarded as systems; for others, they are studied as sub-systems of a larger complex. An aggregate of schools and colleges can usefully be regarded as a system for some purposes, though it is clearly a sub-system of a comprehensive educational system, which itself is a sub-system of a larger politico-social system. In ascending order of complexity, the systems studied in educational research comprise:

(i) the individual components of an educational system or some particular aspect of these components;
(ii) the educational system in its entirety;
(iii) the educational system and its components in relationship to socio-economic and other factors. In this area, especially, educational research for obvious reasons is multidisciplinary in character.

The Figure 6.1 takes us a stage further in elaborating the concept of system, as applied to education. In this figure, the basic system is depicted as consisting of :

1. inputs (students needing education);
2. processes (education provided by institutions);
3. outputs (educated persons); and
4. feedback (effects of processes on future inputs),

operating within a number of constraints, such as buildings, equipment, geography, and population distribution.

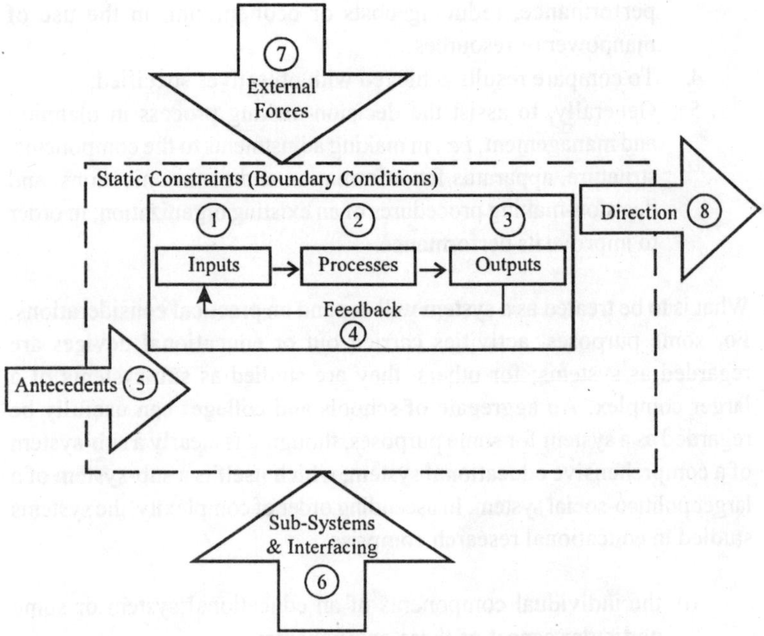

Fig. 6.1: The Concept of System, as Applied to Educaiton

This system, represented diagramatically as:

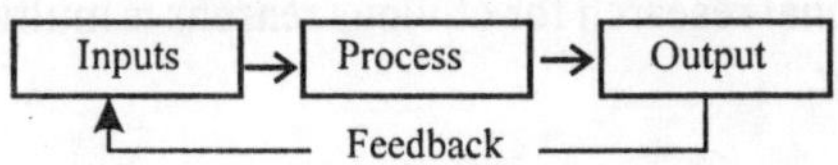

is the prototype operational system. For greater clarity, forces acting upon the prototype, as they relate to education, are shown below:

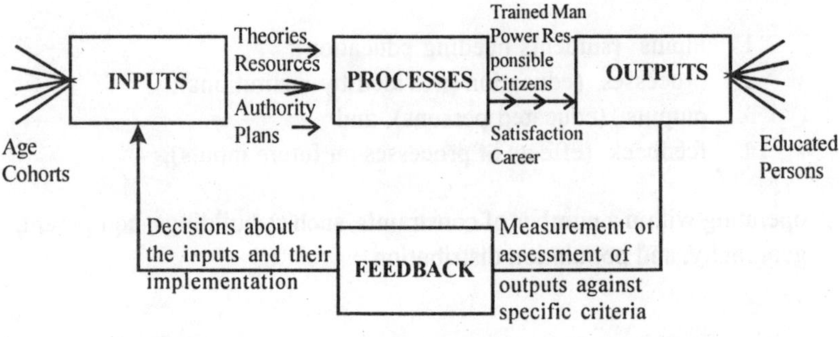

REFINING THE PLAN

The Systems Analysis approach, as described above, is an example of the several "constructive" techniques currently in use for sketching the operating features of a plan. To refine the plan "interrogative" techniques, such as Interpretive Structural Modeling (ISM), simulation and other mathematical techniques are applied to reveal ways that the plan can be improved. These techniques permit the planner to interrogate the model of the plan in order to explore how changes in assumptions, resources, and the like, influence its efficiency, effectiveness and acceptability.

Most interrogative techniques focus on how inputs are transformed to an output. These techniques offer ways to shape system procedures. Interrogative techniques are used for all projects that demand quality as an outcome. In all other projects, the demands made on the planning process do not warrant the use of interrogative techniques. The transforming mechanism can be adequately detailed in the constructive phase.

INTERPRETIVE STRUCTURAL MODELING

Interpretive Structural Modeling (ISM) uses notions of graph theory to create a network which describes the relational properties among a set of elements. The ISM procedure has two key steps: constructing an element set and specifying relation among the elements. The elements correspond to "nodes" in a network and the relationship between elements is denoted graphically by a line segment. With such a model, the planner can focus attention on the logic of each relationship, questioning and fine-tuning it. The ability to interrogate the model without losing sight of the overall structure is a key element, and benefit of ISM.

PATH TECHNIQUES

Path techniques can be used to control, manipulate, or study a sequence of well defined activities. They can be used in tandem with the ISM technique or separately, where the sequence of activities in a transform are well known.

Charting Techniques

Laying out the time relationship among activities helps to find gaps in

the logic. Two simple devices are often used: Gantt charts and Milestone charts. The Gantt chart is used for planning, control, and to demarcate progress toward a goal. As a planning device, bars are placed on a chart to describe all events needed to convert inputs to outputs, against processing time. An example is shown in Figure 6.2. The total processing cycle in this case would be *n* time increments. In this example, there are four tasks. C is dependent upon the completion of B while B and D can begin earlier.

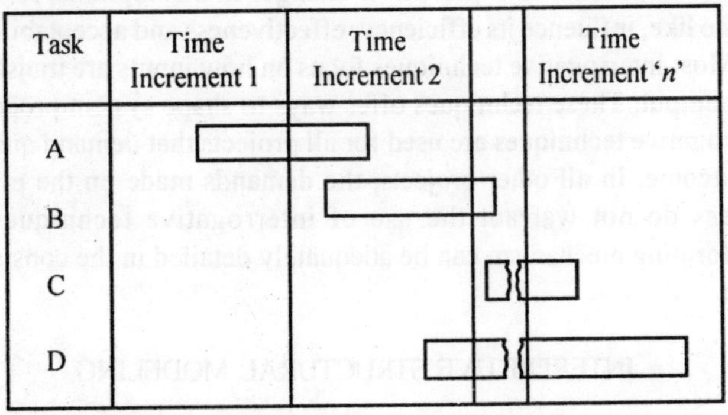

Fig. 6.2: A Gantt Chart for Planning

Milestone charts are used to show the control and reporting points within a sequence of activities. As such they represent a refinement to a Gantt chart. Milestone charts are used primarily to show when needed control reports should be provided and to suggest the information they should contain. An example is provided in Figure 6.3.

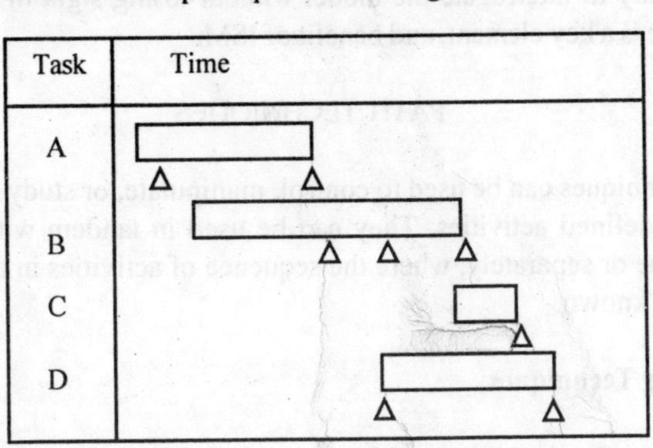

Fig. 6.3: Milestone Chart (The triangle designates a control point)

Network Techniques

Networks can be used both to represent and analyze a sequence of tasks. Programme Evaluation and Review Technique (PERT) and the Critical Path Method (CPM) consider the time needed to carry out steps in a process, constructing a network which links the steps. For example, the steps for food preparation in a school or college cafeteria can be laid out by observing the food service activities (or those in comparable institutions). The network finds the "critical path" of steps. To reduce food preparation time, activities along this path are studied in an attempt to shorten them.

The two procedures, PERT and CPM, were introduced at approximately the same time. Each can be used to represent the steps used to convert input(s) to output(s). The steps are called "activities". The CPM activities as shown in Figure 6.4, are denoted by arrows and the boxes that connect the arrows are called "events", representing points in time when an activity is completed.

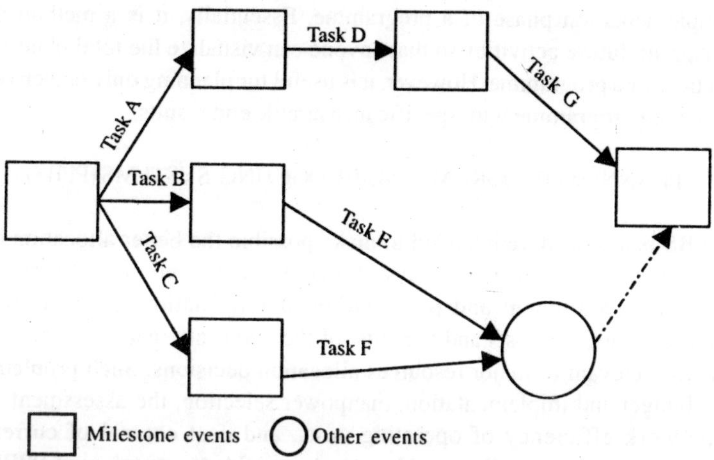

Fig. 6.4: CPM Network

A typical PERT diagram is shown in Figure 6.5. The PERT on occasion must use "dummy" activities (arrows) to show the dependency of one step on another. The CPM does not use dummy activities, which some consider an advantage. However, tracing paths through the network is harder with CPM because the linkages are not as clear.

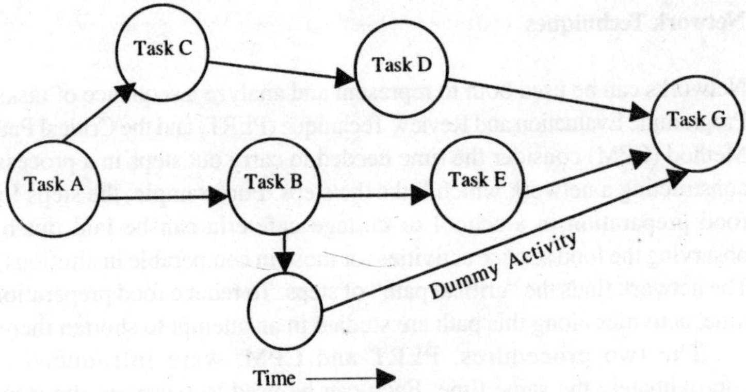

Fig. 6.5: PERT Network

PERT is adapted from the work-flow studies long used in industrial management. Proceeding on the basis that the relations within the planning process are dynamic, it provides a graphic detailed representation of the components of a programme. It is most useful when planning the implementation phase of a programme. Essentially, it is a method of mapping future activities so that anyone can visualize the total plans of action for a programme. However, it is useful for planning only objective-oriented programme with specific measurable end results.

PLANNING-PROGRAMMING-BUDGETING SYSTEMS (PPBS)

PPBS is a procedure intended to make possible the better allocation of resources among alternate ways of attaining a desired object. It relies on the development and presentation of information as to the full implications, the costs and benefits, of the major alternative courses of action relevant to major resources allocation decisions. Such problems as budget and implementation, manpower selection, the assessment of the work efficiency of operating units, and cost control of current operations are generally considered to be outside the purview of PPBS. Cost accounting and non-fiscal performance reporting systems are very important in providing basic data required for PPBS analyses. However, such systems are usually considered complementary to PPBS rather than directly part of it. The main contribution of PPBS lies in the planning process, *i.e.*, the process of making programme policy decisions that lead to a specific budget and specify multi-years plans.

OPERATIONS RESEARCH

Operations research originated from the efforts of scientists of many disciplines to solve military operations problems during World War II. It is a term applied to research into some or all aspects of conducting or operating a system, a business, or a service, while treating the system as a living organism in its proper environment. Its major phases are as follows:

1. Formulating the problem, including definition of the objectives.
2. Collection of data relevant to the problem.
3. Analysis of data to produce a hypothesis and a mathematical model to represent the system under study.
4. Deriving solutions from the model.
5. Choosing the optimal solution and forecasting results.
6. Testing the optimal combination of interventions.
7. Recommending implementation of the solution.

EVALUATION PROCESS

Planning without implementation leads to nothing, and implementation without evaluation can conceivably make matters even worse. On the contrary, in a conscientiously conducted evaluation process, the most valuable insights are gained concerning ways in which planning can be improved and performance upgraded. While this endorsement of evaluation is perhaps as acceptable as any, the fact remains that in practice evaluation is often considered too late and then only lightly.

Role of Evaluation in Planning

Evidently this is the result of failure to understand the important roles of evaluation in planning: (a) to provide a means for continuing self-study and (b) to offer periodic external review. No one enjoys being policed; moreover, most of us exhibit greater energy in contemplating the future than in mulling over the past. Thus, when evaluation is looked upon as little more than a search for past failures, it is not surprising that little enthusiasm is generated, especially among those whose wrists may get slapped in the process.

In contrast, when the notion of continuing self-study is recognized to connote current and private surveillance designed to keep an individual

or an agency in line with objectives—or perhaps to help explain why this is impossible to do—then the merits of evaluation begin to be appreciated. Further, when the review of accomplishments is designed for future improvement as well as past assessment, evaluation is likely to become still more palatable.

Scope of Evaluation

Related to the role of evaluation is its scope. In the strictest sense it asks: what *has been* done? More dynamically, however, it asks: what *is being* done? Most appropriately it enters the scene early to ask: what *can be* done?

When we seek to know what has been done, we are really drawing attention to two considerations. First, we are implying that a problem existed that reflected a sufficient departure from some norm to be considered important. Thus, inherent in evaluation is the notion of problems, goals and priorities. Second, action to alleviate the problem is implied. Hence, evaluation inherently involves a measurement of resources and activities. Presumably these resources and activities are embodied within particular organizational relationships and responsibilities. The true importance of organizational inter-relationships is recognized, however, only when we express the more dynamic concern for what is being done. The evaluation begins to incorporate the notions of feedback, adjustment and adaptability. Finally, when evaluation enters the picture early enough to consider what can be done, we sense the availability and the importance of controllable alternatives in place of the fatalistic recording of accomplished fact.

General Principles of Evaluation

Here are a number of principles of evaluation which must be recognized and enunciated:

(a) Evaluation must be *forward looking* recognizing that planning, implementation, evaluation, and control comprise a unified dynamic feedback mechanism rather than a series of independent stages of a process. The evaluation aspect must be continuing and productive of guidelines for future changes as well as a record of past accomplishments and failures.

(b) Evaluation must exhibit adequate concern for the *relationship*

between ends and means. If implementation consists of the mobilization of resources and activities to accomplish certain objectives, then evaluation must incorporate measurements both of the levels of input (*i.e.*, the action taken) and of output (*i.e.*, performance).

(c) To be effective, evaluation must relate to the *centralization-decentralization* dilemma. When we add to the second point above recognition that action is taken through organization, evaluation clearly must be focused upon areas of responsibility. The advantages of decentralization can be fulfilled only to the extent that standards and measurements are feasible. Under such conditions the evaluation mechanism can be sufficiently powerful that the span of control can be loosened and lenghthened.

(d) Effective evaluation depends upon the existence of a good *information system*. Good information systems are not automatically those that produce the greatest volume of data. Indeed, as evaluation programmes are extended the danger is that increased demands for information will be self-defeating. Instead, great care must be exercised to provide for the acquisition of limited amounts of truly useful information at the *right place* and the *right time*.

Specific Elements of Evaluation

Turning to the more specific elements of evaluation programme in practice, we identify four basic aspects: appropriateness, adequacy, effectiveness, and efficiency.

(a) *Appropriateness* comes into focus first as one asks critically whether the contemplated programme is really directed at an important problem. Superficially, this appraisal may appear to be quite straight forward, but in fact, it is sometimes difficult to be objective with respect to parochial interests that carry the ability to marshal a seemingly strong case and to present it vigorously. On the other hand, a good argument can be made for permitting a highly qualified and motivated organization to tackle a problem of only moderate community importance rather than to assign an important task to an indifferent agency with talents foreign to the job.

(b) Once it is clear that attention is indeed being directed toward a problem of considerable magnitude, the question arises whether the contemplated programme is *adequate* to make much of a difference. This aspect of evaluation is simply the determination of whether the mountain is to be removed through the use of teaspoons or bulldozers. Alternatively, it serves to guard against the attempt to assemble fine watches with the aid of pipe wrenches and sledge hammers.

(c) The third aspect of evaluation, *effectiveness,* lies at the heart of the present discussion. Effectiveness can be defined as the extent to which pre-established objectives are attained as a result of activity.

(d) Programme *efficiency* in turn is defined as the cost of resources of attaining objectives. Together, effectiveness and efficiency make up programme performance. Thus, shortcomings in performance can be analyzed to determine the extent to which inputs, regardless of how efficiently mobilized, failed to produce the anticipated results.

Finally, the evaluation measurements must be *timely* to be really worthwhile, and they must be made at the critical points in the programme.

TECHNICAL-VOCATIONAL EDUCATION AND THE PLANNING PROCESS

Planning in technical-vocational education assumes a peculiar bent. It is inextricably linked here with the process of career development. Technical-vocational programmes must be planned so that individual are placed on long-range career trajectories in order to enhance individual lifelong employability and earnings. This objective requires an understanding of career formation in various parts of the labour market. Workers must have sufficient transferable skills to permit both successful adaption to shifts in the structure of employment and individual progress through promotions to higher levels on their career paths.

The success of job preparation programme can be measured in terms of their ability to place individuals in jobs that offer stable employment on career ladders. The long-range employment and earnings of an individual trainee, as well as the immediate post-training employment experience, are important factors in evaluating the success of education and training efforts.

For youths a first job rarely establishes a career pattern. Placement in a job does not assure stable employment. On the other hand, many young workers gain primary career jobs only after a number of relatively short term, unstable jobs in the secondary labour market. These jobs serve to develop a record of experience and to orient young workers to the disciplines and behavioural patterns that are associated with success in adult careers. To evaluate the success of schooling and job-related training in channeling young workers into good career opportunities, therefore, graduates should be monitored for an extended period of time, through several jobs, and perhaps over several year.

If career success of graduates is a primary focus of technical-vocational programmes, these programmes must be based on a clear understanding of the available career alternatives.

Some career structures are based on advancement within individual occupations. The crafts and a variety of professional-technical fields require a stable set of occupation-specific skills for which pre-employment training, either in schools or in apprenticeship-type programmes is often appropriate.

However, a much larger number of career opportunities are not tied to a single, clearly defined set of occupational skills. Even for individuals whose career advancement takes place within a single firm, dramatic changes in skill requirements and occupation may occur over time. For these career tracks, job preparation requires an entirely different approach. Employees who fill higher-level positions through internal promotions and on-the-job training look in the hiring process for workers who can be trained and retrained easily and who are least likely to quit once training investments have been made. In this case broad educational and skill competencies are important; particularly entry-level job skills often are not. Prior job experience is often an extremely important factor in gaining access to these career opportunities because evidence of actual job performance and stability are the best signals a prospective employer can obtain of the trainability, work attitudes, and long-run employment potential of a job applicant.

In preparing individuals for careers of this type, any jobs that establish a favourable employment record are helpful, regardless of their particular skill content. For this reason youths who take part-time jobs while still in school tend to be among those who have the greatest career success as adults. These jobs, generally in the secondary labour market, form a kind of bridge between schooling and careers, which needs to be better understood in career planning.

Pre-employment vocational preparation for career opportunities in internal labour markets, as well as a number of other career paths involving frequent occupational changes, often requires only very basic skill development. Employers generally identify five categories of skills their workers must have: communication and computational skills, interpersonal skills, productive work attitudes, a familiarity with the world of work, and basic occupational skills. For many entry-level positions, occupational skill requirements are minimal and may be too plant-specific to serve as prerequisites to hiring. Many employers seek the array of other skills, instead, in screening job candidates for long-term positions in the firm.

This view of career formation suggests an approach to technical-vocational education that is in sharp contrast to the prevailing one. With few exceptions, job-specific skills should be taught prior to employment only for positions on occupation-based career ladders, where the markets for these skills are relatively robust. Ideally, training should depend on prior hiring commitments by the relevant local employers. Alternatively, clear evidence should be available that employment is likely for the programme graduates once they have acquired the occupation-specific skills. When actual jobs are not identified, training should be as widely transferable as possible and care should be taken to assure that employer screens will not automatically exclude programme trainees regardless of their skill attainments.

The focus on careers cannot stop with the initial entry of workers into jobs. Ongoing retraining opportunities should be available to allow for individual career changes and to accommodate the changing skill needs of the economy over time. Whether they are caused by involuntary dislocations or by individual decisions to seek a more rewarding alternative in the labour market, midcareer changes often involve serious financial and psychological setbacks. Without effective retraining opportunities and support in these transitions, individual hardships may be severe.

Planning for both occupation-specific training programmes and placement of individuals on the broader array of career tracks in the labour market requires better labour market information than has been provided by local employment forecasts. Employment projections are least accurate at the local level and shed little light on the job opportunities to which new labour market entrants may have access. More detailed information concerning employer hiring practices is required. The subset of jobs that are staffed in the open labour market

and the smaller number of jobs for which recent vocational trainees are likely to be eligible need to be identified. Planners of programmes outside the workplace must carefully target education and training toward entry-level jobs that can provide access to viable career ladders for programme graduates. This type of planning, which is essential if technical-vocational programmes are to match individuals with careers more effectively, will require much closer cooperation and coordination between programme planners and employers. Programmes outside the workplace must complement training that is provided directly by employers.

Planners should also consider the special vocational need of women, minorities and handicapped individuals. As career opportunities increase for these segments of the society, institutions of technical-vocational learning should take a lead in preparing them to meet the new challenges. Female and minority students will need current labour market information that accurately reflects job options, as well as counselling and placement assistance in adapting to non-traditional roles and employment in the economy. Institutions should be ready to provide any compensatory education and training that is required to make these transitions successful.

SUMMARY

Planning is making current decisions in the light of their future effects. Educational planning entails producing valid information in the form of alternative courses of action to aid decision-making by those who are concerned with educational policy formulation and administration. There are three types of planning: project planning, systems planning and policy planning—each applied at different levels under different situations.

There are various approaches to planning. In education, especially technical-vocational education, the systems approach to planning has been found to be the most effective one, and hence discussed at greater length in this chapter. PPBS, PERT, ISM, Operations Research and Path Techniques are other notable approaches to planning.

After decisions have been made and the programme is implemented, the return of information about the system as a whole and each of its component parts becomes crucial. Evaluation, just as method analysis, clarification of objectives, and constant review of the other steps in planning, begins with the first step and continues throughout the process. Evaluation must be forward looking, objective, appropriate, adequate, effective, efficient, and timely to have the maximum impact.

Planning of technical-vocational programmes requires special skills. These programmes need to be targeted more carefully toward career-ladder jobs in the adult labour market and must focus more on preparing students to move as efficiently as possible through the process of job search, while they build work experience and move toward adult career ladders. This suggests a greater orientation on widely transferable skills and on a strong foundation in basic communication, computation and interpersonal skills. Plans should also be made to provide students general orientation to the "world of work", improved counselling concerning the relationship between early job experiences and later career options, and better placement services.

7

Economic Dimensions of Administration

Two of the basic functions of an administrator are planning and controlling. Through his planning, he formulates courses of action for the system which he operates. He determines when things should be done and how they should be done. In fact, without administrative planning and controlling, the activities of the various systems of an institution could well develop into a series of random activities with meaningless objectives.

The conduct of a modern comprehensive programme of technical-vocational education involves a large number of business procedures. It is estimated that more than half of a principal's time is devoted to activities related to financial planning and management. They range from participation in budget planning and the purchase of supplies and equipment to the collection of fees and the maintenance of the school building. For the most part, principals have only supplementary and cumulative duties in connection with the general financial operation of their schools. Most fiscal functions are delegated to the superintendent or the accounts officer of the institution, and are performed by him or his central office staff. But, there is recent trend toward more participation by principals and supervisors in these matters, especially in planning the budget.

BUDGET MAKING

The budget is the heart of fiscal management. It is a recorded (written) plan of action. It shows how a future operating period is expected to develop. A budget, however, is usually expressed in quantitative terms. A good school budget relates educational plans to financial plans. It includes long-term and short-term educational plans plus estimates of receipts and expenditures for the next fiscal year and for a period of several years.

As the budget is the fiscal interpretation of the educational programmes, it implies that reducing the proposed expenditures or refusing to approve the procurement of receipts stipulated in the budget has more than merely monetary significance. Such acts affect the quality and quantity of educational services available in the area. In one sense, the budget can be regarded as an expression of the educational hopes and aspirations of the people. It is by nature future oriented.

Budgeting is stimulated by the need for economy and efficiency in financial operations. In this sense the budget becomes a disciplined way to handle school expenditures. It is traditionally conceived as a control device. It appeared in governmental affairs early in the twentieth century, although it was used in private business and industry prior to that time. Local school districts were among the last of the governmental districts to develop and use the budget. Prior to World War I budgetary practices in local school systems were relatively undeveloped and non-standardized. Even at the present time, the recommendations cited in the voluminous literature on this subject have been practiced in only a very limited way. One of the significant contributions of the professionally prepared school superintendents, soon after World War II, was to design and introduce the budget as an important instrument in school operations and to utilize budgeting as a meaningful planning and control process.

The Budgetary Process

The phases in the budgetary process are preparation, presentation, adoption and authorization, administration, execution, and appraisal.

Responsibility for budget preparation rests with the superintendent, or in a large institution, with the assistant superintendent in charge of business services. The three major phases of budget preparation are: (1) determination of the educational programme for the period in question, (2) estimation of expenditures necessary to realize the programme, and (3) estimation of revenues or receipts anticipated from local, state, or central sources. These phases are often referred to, respectively, as the educational plan, the expenditure plan, and the revenue plan. Although there is considerable agreement that the educational plan is the most important part of budget preparation, few executives include the statement of the educational programme to be realized in the budget document. It is difficult to defend a budget request professionally without justification based on educational goals envisioned. The educational plan must be translated into reasonably accurate expenditure estimates. This does not

mean that no consideration is given to the revenue plan until expenditures are known. The three phases of budget preparation are considered at the same time. It can be called as "long-term budgeting", and is one aspect of the Planning-Programming-Budgeting System (PPBS).

The budget document is the general financial and educational plan for a stated period of time. It evolves from continuous fiscal and educational planning. The budget document contains a balanced statement of estimated revenues and estimated expenditures. The justification of anticipated expenditures is based on the desired educational programme. The budget document also includes exhibits that report in some detail the current financial condition of various funds at the start of the fiscal year.

The prepared budget document is submitted to the board of education, which adopts, rejects or modifies it. Presentation of the budget document is an executive activity. Adoption of the budget is a board of education function; authorization of the budget, after review and evaluation, is a legislative function.

Administration of the budget follows approval and authorization. This, again, is an executive activity. The authority to expend the amounts stated in the budget document should be delegated to the chief executive officer of the board of education. So long as he expends funds within budgetary allotments, there should be no need for board approval prior to a purchase. A different set of circumstances prevails when extra-budgetary purchases are envisioned.

Appraisal of the budget document is a function of the board and the superintendent. Primary responsibility, however, rests with the policy-making agency.

The term "balanced budget" is a relative one that means usually an excess of revenues over expenditures. The budget serves as a means of controlling future fiscal operations after the estimated expenditures and receipts have been approved.

The Planning-Programming-Budgeting-System (PPBS)

PPBS is more than a new approach to budgeting. It is a part of what is known as the systems approach to school administration. It thus might be more accurately labelled a "Resource Allocation Decision System" (RADS). PPBS focuses primarily on the educational plan and expenditure plan in budgeting. It ignores the important financing plan (the receipts side) of the budget document.

PPBS is more than a new fiscal instrument, although it does give rise to a different looking budget document. Its primary concern is with expenditures. Though dynamic relations exist among its many dimensions—planning, programming, budgeting, analyzing and evaluating—it focuses on the total configuration of activities. PPBS allows the systematic analysis of alternatives; it provides a way of improving how limited resources are to be allocated among various programmes.

The school's accounts officer and many other second-echelon administrative personnel are involved in several phases of the total PPBS system. It is the general school executive at the top level who directs PPBS rather than the school account official. As an outcomes-oriented management system, the PPBS budget is a planning tool as well as an instrument to control expenditure patterns. It demands inter-relations of key administrators—the team or task force approach—which is basic to systems approach to administration.

Programme Budgeting

Programme budgeting has become a popular term during the last decade. Some use the term as a synonym for PPBS even though the originators of the PPBS seldom mentioned programme budgeting; others insist that the two phrases are not synonymous.

Whether programme budgeting is a more meaningful fiscal analysis and control device, or a comprehensive systems approach, is a matter of definition. For the purpose of this writing, programme budgeting is a subset of the PPBS. It is concerned primarily with developing programmatic classifications for educational budget categories. Its function is to facilitate operations analysis. It focuses on output-oriented categorization of budgets. It involves restructuring budget preparations to reveal outputs as well as inputs and to relate each to objectives.

ACCOUNTING

The system of accounting grows out of the production of records of financial transactions. From the basic documents and their subsequent classification a picture of the educational programme develops as contained in the budget. Accounts reveal changes in financial status of the district. The central aspects of accounting are the maintenance of essential records in which are summarized financial transactions of the

institution and the reporting and interpretation of them. Accounting involves recording, classifying, summarizing, and reporting in terms of money, the activities and events affecting the financial character of the administrative unit and its programmes. The exact records to be kept and the manner in which fiscal information is to be classified and summarized depends upon: (1) the purposes of the institution, (2) the financial information required for prudent administration, and (3) the principles and practices of accounting. There is no one set of records or one type of book-keeping procedure that must be employed in all types of institutions. Although some principles and standards apply both to public school and commercial accounting, there are fundamental differences between the two.

Computer-based electronic devices promise to facilitate school-accounting procedures in small and large districts alike. The advent of machines makes it difficult to justify the keeping of only minimum or inadequate financial records on the grounds that too many workers are needed to discharge financial responsibilities adequately.

Purposes of Accounting

Purposes of school accounting are:

1. To safeguard school-district funds from loss, theft, waste or misuse.
2. To promote budgetary control.
3. To provide information to management that is necessary in policy formulation.
4. To provide information necessary to the public and the school board to appraise the management of the local school system.
5. To provide data required for state reports.
6. To show that legal mandates have been complied with.

If financial information among communities in various states or provinces is to be comparable, there is a need for uniformity in terminology in accounting. Also, if operations analysis and cost-effectiveness studies are to be possible in education, present accounting systems must be re-designed, in terms of outputs rather than inputs, to permit establishment of the PPBS.

FUND ACCOUNTING

As indicated previously, a fund does not refer to money itself, but an independent accounting for specific activities that may be related to the attainment of objectives. Some of the most commonly seen funds in educational institutions are: General Fund, Special Revenue Fund, Debt Service Fund, Capital Projects Fund and Pupil Activity Fund.

Receipt Accounts

Various funds and receipt accounts which are universally seen are identified in this section. A fund is a sum of money or other financial resources segregated for specified activities within limits set by laws or regulations. Thus, each fund must be an independent fiscal and accounting entity. Any fund can be divided into a number of accounts for the purpose of systematizing financial transactions. Those financial transactions related to receiving money are classified as receipt accounts; those related to spending as expenditure accounts.

The receipt accounts for public schools can be classified as revenue-receipt accounts, non-revenue-receipt accounts, and incoming-transfer accounts.

Revenue-receipt accounts record money that increases assets without increasing school indebtedness by reducing the value of, or by depleting, school property. Included is revenue from local sources, from intermediate governmental units, from state sources, and from Central Government sources. Most of the tax funds and grants received are classified in revenue-receipts accounts.

Non-revenue-receipt accounts record money produced as a result of incurring an obligation to the district which must be amortized at some future date or money produced from the sale of school property. In such accounts are recorded sale of school bonds, loans and similar financial transactions. The term "non-revenue" appears contradictory if revenue is equated with money, and "non-revenue" receipts is translated as "non-money" receipts. A better term is needed, but for the present, non-revenue applies to a type of receipt.

Incoming-transfer accounts record money received from other school districts for services rendered. Included are tuition receipts, which could distort the picture of total school receipts in a state or nation if they were not identified by the special terminology. Incoming-transfer accounts avoid duplication of data on school receipts and, therefore, ensure more reliable and more comparable state and national figures on receipts.

Clearing Accounts

Clearing accounts or "revolving funds" record gross amounts of money received for various school activities and allowed to accumulate for a specified period of time before being disbursed or distributed to appropriate agencies or other accounts. In the conduct of school business affairs certain financial transactions involve a double handling of money. To illustrate, money may be received from the operation of a given activity and then spent again for the same activity in a cycle of operations. Recording these activities in regular receipts and expenditure accounts would greatly distort financial operations.

Clearing accounts are used when the single-entry system of book-keeping is employed. They are not required in the double-entry system; in the double-entry system a profit-loss statement is prepared and either profit or loss is transferred to another fund at the end of a given accounting period.

Expenditure Accounts

Schools incur liabilities through the purchase of materials and supplies and through contracts for personal services. It is necessary in all school systems to purchase and manage school supplies and equipment with the greatest amount of efficiency, so that loss or misuse will be minimized. Procurement of school materials begins with a requisition, a request by the teacher for approval of the purchase of supplies and equipment. It in turn leads to the purchase order, a document authorizing the seller to deliver the described merchandise or material at a specified price. When accepted by the seller, the purchase order becomes a contract. After materials specified have been shipped to the school system, the seller submits an invoice, a document calling for payment for merchandise delivered. The invoice activates expenditure of funds from the school treasury.

Encumbrance Accounts

Encumbrance accounting is rapidly becoming an important part of school fiscal management. There is a difference between an encumbrance and an expenditure. An encumbrance is a commitment of resources prior to actual disbursement of funds to liquidate a liability. It ensures that the money cannot be used for anything else until the expenditure has been realized. Encumbrance accounting enables a school district to know

how much money has been spent or has been committed to be spent at any given time. Without encumbrance accounting, the exact financial situation at any period of time can only be estimated.

AUDITING

The audit is a systematic investigation, verification, and critical review of financial operations of an organization. Its primary function is to verify the financial status of the organization.

Audits may be classified as general or special audits, or complete or limited audits. A general audit is concerned with all fiscal transactions and records for every school fund; it is a comprehensive review. A special audit is limited to a particular aspect of school fiscal transaction. A complete audit is a thorough analysis of operations, necessitating a careful study of the system of internal control and of all books and accounts, including subsidiary records and supporting documents. A limited audit reviews only selective items; it is based on sampling rather than a complete review of every financial transaction. There are complete general audits, limited general audits, complete special audits and limited special audits. A complete general audit checks all funds and is based on an intensive examination and verification of all items during a given account period. A complete special audit is concerned only with specific parts of the school's financial operations.

Pre-audits, continuous audits, and post-audits are classifications based on time. A pre-audit is an investigation and critical review prior to consummation of a transaction. It is a means of avoiding expenditures of borderline validity and preventing money appropriated for one purpose from being used for another. Pre-auditing takes place in the normal careful accounting routine when this involves the checking of an expenditure to ascertain that it is authorized in a budget and that unencumbered funds are available. A post-audit takes place after the transaction has been completed. It is the most common type audit and is frequently referred to as the "annual school audit" . The most common type of audit required by government law is the annual independent audit, which is a post-audit.

An auditor functions most effectively as an expert in accounting or auditing and least effectively as an expert in educational philosophy and curriculum. Educational policy should never be exercised through school audits.

There is evidence to indicate the need for improvement in school-district audit laws. Relatively few laws stipulate the time and scope of the

audit, or the qualifications of the school auditor. The schools sometimes don't abide by the suggestions of the audit report and often there is no follow up.

COST ACCOUNTING AND UNIT-COST ANALYSIS

The purpose of unit-cost analysis are to ascertain the costs of operating a given school facility, to judge the efficiency and practicality of certain school activities, to help in the budgeting of activities that can be reduced to measurable units, to estimate costs of proposed projects, and to compare educational costs among communities. Perhaps the most dangerous of these steps is the comparison. The temptation to analyze the cost of educational programmes is very great despite the many chances of misinterpretation.

One difficulty in unit-cost analysis is ascertaining appropriate units of measurement. Unless units are comparable for the area under investigation, unit-cost analysis is of questionable value. Cost accounting for schools endeavours to ascertain and evaluate the cost of operating various phases of the educational experience. It is limited by the financial information available and the design of procedures in accounting. A well-designed and well-kept accounting system will facilitate the gathering of cost data but cannot guarantee correct interpretation of such information.

Unit-cost figures for different school systems should be qualified if they are not based on the same educational programme. It is erroneous to assume that the same educational programme is being purchased with the same or differing amounts of money in all school systems. The selection of appropriate units for cost analysis compounds the problem. Cost accounting may be confused with cost effectiveness or cost-utility analysis. The last two terms are related to the systems approach to administration and involve far and more than unit cost analysis. The cost-accounting procedures may provide basic data in the cost-effectiveness analysis.

FINANCIAL REPORTING

Financial reports are a means of informing the school board, professional administrators, and public and state officials of the fiscal state of the school. Reports are prepared on a monthly, quarterly, or annual basis. Some reflect the status of receipts and expenditures; others are concerned

with the general financial condition of the school system. It is usually the function of the school superintendent to prepare the financial reports. The form and content of a report vary with its purpose. The systems approach requires reporting by outputs as well as inputs.

School records accumulate fast, and there is a need for legislation and policy to determine which records should be kept and which destroyed. The cost of storing records is quite high in modern times. As long as there are no statutory requirements to the contrary, many school records and reports can be disposed of after ten years without adversely affecting school administration.

ACCOUNTING FOR SCHOOL PROPERTY

An educational institution, with all its movable and immovable property, is a tremendous investment that must be safeguarded and carefully identified with a system of property accounting.

The status of school property accounting is decades behind that of accounting for other school financial transactions. Inadequate property records characterize most educational institutions. This is in stark contrast with the capital-accounting procedures in a business or industry. Property accounting for schools is necessary, but for different reasons than those which prompt it in the business and in the commercial world.

A property account can be defined as a descriptive heading under which is posted specific information about land improvements and building and equipment owned/or controlled by the school district. The term "account" is used in the sense of a formal record rather than a descriptive classification of a financial transaction.

The various types of property accounts can be classified under the following headings:

1. Type of plant (elementary, secondary, or other used for instructional or non-instructional purposes).
2. Land facilities.
3. Improvements to school sites.
4. Building facilities (type, kind, cost and size of building).
5. Equipment (instructional as well as non-instructional).

PROTECTION OF SCHOOL PERSONNEL AND PROPERTY

At one time attacks on teachers and vandalism of educational property

were a rarity or not a significant concern. This changed dramatically during the last two decades. The school administrator is now confronted with the challenge of making the school a secure place. In doing so, he or she finds insurance as a useful tool.

Insurance affords protection against financial loss from loss of life, crime, destruction of property or other causes. In return for a relatively small payment—a premium—that is collected from many individuals, a company assumes risk of the possibility of a substantial, even though unknown, financial loss to each party who pays a premium. Insurance companies are professional risk bearers. Insurance is a means of gaining some measure of financial security even though catastrophe may strike.

The major classifications for insurance are property, liability, crime, and personal welfare. Property insurance gives security against financial loss from property damage or destruction arising from fire, floods, storms, explosions etc. Liability insurance provides some measures of security to the insured if his unintentional acts injure or damage another person's body or property. Crime insurance protects against financial loss through the commission by others or intentional and illegal acts such as robbery, theft, and embezzlement. The various types of health, accident, and life policies constitute personal-welfare insurance. With the exception of the last mentioned, schools are well advised to contribute to all.

CALCULATION OF THE COST OF A TRAINING PROGRAMME

There will be occasions when the administrator of a technical-vocational institution will have to decide upon the economic feasibility of instituting a new programme, continuing a programme already in existence, or letting it discontinue. At times, and at a higher level, he may have to choose a particular type of training method from among the basic methods now used widely: training on the job; training off the job in schools, training centres, or places of work; and combined types of training such as apprenticeship, on-the-job training with some related instruction and cooperative work training.

Each method offers certain advantages and disadvantages. With on-the-job training the trainee is assured a job and income, and does not have to be concerned about finding work after finishing the course. This type of training is feasible only when there are job openings and the ratio of trainees to employees is small. Another limitation is that the training might focus on a narrowly defined skill that cannot be used in other occupations.

Classroom training whether in schools, factories or training centres, has the advantages of accommodating a large number of students and offering a variety of courses: full or part time, throughout the day and week. The drawbacks are that it requires a minimum number of students and trained instructors. Such programmes tend to become inflexible, especially when expensive equipment is needed, and there is no guarantee of employment after the course is completed.

Apprenticeship is sometimes the only way to acquire the needed credentials for a job, but the training period may be unduly long. Cooperative work-study programmes provide income and experience while allowing the trainees to finish high school, but they require close coordination of the roles of schools and employers. The benefits of other combined methods of training are similarly balanced by certain drawbacks.

Of all the methods available the favourite choice of developing countries is the vocational school. It offers the most accessible type of training and is the least encumbered by administrative and operational obstacles.

Before more resources are poured into vocational schools, however, some basic questions need to be answered: Is this the most effective type of training? How do costs compare with those of other methods? Can other programmes be readily substituted for vocational schools?

In industrial countries it is generally believed that costs of formal vocational training are higher than those of on-the-job training—although a detailed study in West Germany shows the opposite to be true.[1] At the same time the training given by vocational schools is believed to be more effective than that received on the job.

Most studies done in developing nations compare the cost effectiveness of vocational and academic secondary schools and generally conclude that vocational schools are not profitable. This could be the result of inefficient operations, but it is believed to be primarily because there is little demand in the labour market for the training which was received. If, as some studies find, many vocational school graduates do not find jobs, is that because of faulty instruction or because they were trained for the wrong occupation? In the latter case a different mode of training would not alter the result unless the decision-making process that determines the content of instruction is corrected to conform with market conditions. In any event correcting the decision-making process may be cheaper than changing modes of training.

In other studies formal vocational schools show a high cost per graduate.[2] This could result from a poor use of capacity and does not validate a claim that training outside of school is more profitable (assuming

equal benefits). With a more efficient use of faculty and equipment the cost per student could change radically.

All this seems to indicate that it is hard to rely upon any previous research as conditions differ from place to place, and from time to time. For determining the cost-effectiveness of a particular training method the administrator must employ standard methods of calculation that are suitable to his own milieu. An attempt is made below to familiarize the administrator with a few important formulae to estimate the costs of a training programme. The discussion relates to calculating the cost of training in a hypothetical programme—*programme x*—that is being offered in conjunction with other programmes. The entire instruction for programme x is assumed to take place in the course of a year.

Administrative Costs

Administrative costs to be allocated to programme x can be calculated by using the following formula:

$$ADM_x = TCA \times \frac{HRS_x}{\Sigma HRS_j}$$

where

ADM_x = administration cost allocated to programme x
TCA = total costs of administration
HRS_x = student hours of programme x
ΣHRS_j = student hours of all programmes.

Cost of Laboratory Instruction

Laboratory instruction costs to be allocated to programme x can be computed by using the following formula:

$$CLI_{kx} = TCLI_k \times \frac{HRSL_{xk}}{\Sigma HRSL_k}$$

where

CLI_{kx} = cost of laboratory instruction k in programme x
$TCLI_k$ = total cost of laboratory instruction k
$HRSL_{xk}$ = student hours of programme x spent in laboratory k
$\Sigma HRSL_k$ = total student hours of all programmes spent in laboratory k.

Cost of Class Instruction

Class instruction costs to be allocated to programme x can be figured in the following manner:

$$\text{CCI}_x = \text{TCCI} \times \frac{\text{HRSCI}_x}{\Sigma_j \text{HRSCI}_j}$$

where

CCI_x = cost of class instruction in programme x

TCCI = total cost of class instruction

HRSCI_x = student hours of programme x spent in classroom

$\Sigma_j \text{HRSCI}_j$ = student hours of all programme spent in classroom.

Equipment Costs

The cost of equipment can be computed by using the following formula:

$$\text{EC}_x = \sum_{k=1}^{m} \text{TLC}_k \times \frac{\text{H}_{kx} \times \frac{\text{S}_x}{\text{SS}_{ix}}}{\sum_{x=1}^{n} \text{H}_{kx} \times \frac{\text{S}_x}{\text{SS}_{ix}}}$$

where

EC_x = cost of equipment for programme x

TLC_k = total cost of equipment for laboratory k

H_{kx} = total number of instructional hours spent in laboratory k by student in programme x

S_x = number of students in programme x. This is the number of students that will be trained on the equipment over its lifetime, not the number of students in programme x in a given year.

SS_{ix} = student stations per unit of equipment i

$$\text{m} = \frac{\sum_{x=1}^{m} \text{H}_{ks}\text{S}_x}{\text{class size} \times \text{duration of class (in hours)}}$$

and

$$TLC_k = \sum_{i=1}^{V_i} EC_{ik} + FC_k$$

where

EC_{ik} = equipment cost of item *i* used in laboratory *k*

FC_k = fixed costs of laboratory *k* (equipment needed to support machines on which students learn)

and

EC_{ik} = $V_i \times C_i$

where

V_i = number of machines of type *i*

C_i = unit cost of machine *i*

and

$$V_i = \frac{\sum_{x=1}^{m} HRS_{ix} \times \frac{S_x}{SS_{ix}}}{HRSA_i \times u_i}$$

where

HRS_{ix} = hours of instruction on machine *i* required by a student in programme *x*

$HRSA_i$ = hours available on machine *i*

u_i = utilization factor of machine *i*.

Cost of Facilities

The total construction cost allocated to programme x ($TCCP_x$) is:

$$TCCP_x = \sum_{k=1}^{m} TLCC_k \times \frac{H_{kx} \times S_x}{\sum_{x=1}^{n} H_{kx} \times S_x} + TCICC \times \frac{HRSCl_x}{\sum_{x=1}^{n} HRSCl_x}(1+BF)$$

where

$TLCC_k$ = total construction cost of laboratory *k*

TCICC = total classroom construction cost

BF = building factor (allowance to cover overhead space, hallways, offices, washrooms etc.) which ranges between 0.4 and 0.6

$TLCC_k$ = $AREA_k \times CPA_k$

$TClCC = AREA_{cl} \times CPA_{cl}$
$AREA_k$ = area of laboratory k
$AREA_{cl}$ = area of classrooms
CPA_k = construction cost per unit of laboratory k area
CPA_{cl} = construction cost per unit of classroom area.

Annual Variable Costs per Student

To calculate the annual average operating cost per student of programme x, the following formula is used:

$$OCPS_x = \frac{ADM_x + CClI_x + CLI_x + C_m}{NOS_x}$$

where
$OCPS_x$ = total operating cost per student of programme x
ADM_x = administrative cost of programme x
CLI_x = cost of laboratory instruction of programme x
$CClI_x$ = cost of classroom instruction of programme x
C_m = cost of materials
NOS_x = number of programme x students a year.

Annual Fixed Cost

The annual average fixed cost per student of programme x can be calculated as follows:

$$AFCPS_x = \frac{TCCP_x - FRV + EC_x}{TNOS_x}$$

where
$AFCPS_x$ = allocated fixed cost per student in programme x.
$TNOS_x$ = total number of students in programme x over the life of the programme (if the programme is planned for 7 years, then $TNOS_x = 7 \times NOS_x$, or number of students)
$TCCP_x$ = total construction cost for programme x
FRV = facility recovery value (salvage value) after programme x is discontinued.

Total annual average cost per student in programme x ($ACPT_x$) then becomes :

$$ACPT_x = OCPS_x + AFCPS_x$$

Capacity Utilization of Facilities, Equipment and Personnel

Capacity utilization is a relative concept; it is the actual use of capacity as a percentage of a normal measure of capacity. For example, normal capacity of a laboratory may be 30 hours a week multiplied by the number of students that can be taught effectively at one time in the laboratory. Normal instructor capacity might be 15 students multiplied by five hours daily. Given the type of laboratories and programmes in the school, the hours of laboratory and class instruction, and the number of students in each programme it is possible to calculate utilization of capacity. For example:

$$\text{Utilization of Laboratory Capacity} = \frac{\sum_{k=1}^{m} \sum_{x=1}^{n} HRS_{kx}}{\sum_{k=1}^{m} HRS_{nk}}$$

where

HRS_{kx} = hours in laboratory *k* spent by students in programme *x*

HRS_{nk} = normal capacity in student hours of laboratory *k*.

Capacity utilization of teachers can be approximated by the student-teacher ratios of classroom and laboratories separately. In general, utilization of less than 70 per cent of normal capacity should encourage a revision of the programme or of the number of students in it.

Rate of Return for Programme *x*

The rate of return is usually calculated on the basis of occupational earnings by age, adjusted by the probability of employment. These data are not readily available in many developing nations. Moreover, the soundness of using present earnings of older people to represent future earnings of today's entrants to the labour market is highly questionable. It is, therefore, advisable to confine the computations to earnings for the first five years from occupations obtainable after training and those that workers would have held without training. It can be assumed that the difference between the earnings of the two types of occupations remains constant thereafter. The rate of return can be calculated with the following equation:

$$I_{tv} = \frac{E_{tv1} - E_{w1}}{(1+r)} + \frac{E_{tv2} - E_{w2}}{(1+r)^2} + \ldots + \frac{E_{tv5} - E_{w5}}{(1+r)^5} + \ldots + \frac{E_{tvn} - E_{wn}}{(1+r)^n}$$

where

I_{tv} = investment in technical-vocational training
E_{t1} = earnings of an individual with training in year 1
E_{w1} = earnings of an individual without training in year 1.

Data on earnings can be obtained from interviews in a few typical plants, employment exchanges, or labour unions.

Cost per Graduate of Technical-Vocational and Academic Schools

In many developed and developing countries graduates from the academic stream compete successfully for jobs with graduates from technical-vocational schools. In this case, if the type of student input is similar for both schools a comparison of the cost per graduate may provide a clue to the economic viability of technical-vocational education. In general, it should be expected that education in technical-vocational schools is more expensive than in regular academic schools. When the discrepancy is more than 30 per cent, however, a closer scrutiny of the technical-vocational programmes must be made.

SUMMARY

Schools consume resources in the pursuit of objectives. All goals in the instructional programme carry a price tag. This necessitates the procurement of financial resources, as well as the careful management and control following procurement. These are the economic dimensions of educational administration.

Effective fiscal administration is based on budget making, accounting, auditing and financial reporting. The budget is the heart of financial management and is the fiscal translation of the educational programme; the accounts reveal financial status, and the audit verifies its accuracy. All cost accounting depends on the accuracy of financial records. A well-designed and well-kept accounting system will facilitate the gathering of cost data, but cannot guarantee the correct interpretation of such information.

The Planning-Programming-Budgeting-System (PPBS) is the school's part of the systems approach to administration: A fundamental

reorganization of fiscal accounting and budgeting systems and the restatement of objectives for schools will be needed to facilitate the introduction and use of PPBS in education.

The property of a technical-vocational school represents a tremendous investment and should be protected by a system of property accounting. Crime against persons and vandalism of school property are on the increase now. School security has become a major concern for administrators. Property accounting for school lags far behind the recording of other financial transactions. Insurance is protection against the likelihood of financial loss from various sources, and it is a must for educational institutions in order to survive.

Since World War II automation and unemployment in developed countries and the demand for skilled manpower to develop newly founded nations have made it necessary to determine the most effective methods of training. There is a wide array of methods to choose from: training on-the-job; training off-the-job in schools, training centres, or places of work; and combined types of training. More often than not the choice will fall upon the administrator. He should, therefore, be familiar with the techniques of making cost-benefit or cost-effectiveness analyses in order to make a wise choice. This chapter provides methods of calculating the costs of some components that are vital to a training programme in technical-vocational education.

References

1. Winterhager, W.D. *Kosten und Finanzierung der beruflichen bildungeine wirtschaftsheorestische Analyse mit empirichen Daten zur Lehrlingsausbildung in der Industrie* [Theoretical and Empirical Analysis of the Cost of Vocational Training, with particulr reference to the Financial and Input-Output Aspects of Appreticeships in Plant Training]. Stuttgart: Ernst Klett Verlag, 1979.

2. Merenda, P. "the Relative Effectiveness of Formal School and On-the-job Methods of Training Apprentices in Naval Occupations," *Personnel Psychology*, Vol. 11, No. 3, 1968, pp. 379-82, and
Corrazzini, A.J. "The Decision to Invest in Vocational Education: An Analysis of Costs and Benefits," *Journal of Human Resources*, Vol. 3, Supplement, 1968, pp. 38-120.

8

Personnel Management Dimensions of Administration

Administration is often equated with management although there is a distinct difference between the two terms. Administration is that phase of an enterprise which concerns itself with the overall determination of the major policies and objectives. Management is the executive function that concerns itself with the carrying out of the administrative policy laid down by the administration.

Educational administration is that branch of administration which concerns itself with the development of human personality. Although educational administration is a means not an end, still (in spite of the variety of the systems, types and levels of education), there is a universal aim of educational administration. This is to enable the right pupils to receive the right education under the right teacher at the lowest possible cost for the benefit of the community. Obviously, this calls for a high level of managerial skills or expertise in personnel/human resource management.

Personnel or human resources management is a set of organization wide functions or activities that are designed to influence the effectiveness of employees in the organization. Most educational administrators engage in these activities daily with their instructional, clerical, and maintenance staff. In a strict sense personnel management involves a lot of specialized activities which, in a large organization, are in the hands of a qualified personnel officer. However, in the school setting it is usually the administrator who assumes this role.

A good administrator sees his subordinate employees as reliable, trustworthy members of a team of which he is the captain. Like a good captain he instills in them a feelings of trust, security, and belongingness. In return, he expects his teammates to measure upto a desirable level of performance and "deliver the goods". If that does not happen he is not

afraid of applying corrective or even punitive measures. This chapter covers five important aspects of personnel management which would help the school principal, supervisor, or the department head to deal with their subordinates effectively and in an atmosphere of mutual trust.

COMMUNICATION

Communication is the exchange—upward, downward, lateral—of information and ideas. To be successful it must result in a common understanding between all who are part of the communication network. Much of what the administrator or supervisor does in some way resembles what the subordinate does. The key difference between the manager and the worker is that the manager must get work done *through* other people. This can only be accomplished by means of sound communication. Communication is neither an appendage nor an afterthought in the organization's life-style. It is the cornerstone of organizational life and existence. Within the complex organizational patterns of the modern vocational services institution, it is clear that communication programmes must be developed on a sophisticated level with the prime goal of optimizing understanding and effecting maximum cooperation of all levels of staff. Communication grows best in a climate of trust and confidence. An administration that does one thing and says another cannot, in the final analysis, expect communications to be effective.

Planning Communication

The planning of communication is essential to producing the resultant optimum objectives. It is inconceivable to think of any form of interpersonal relationship and activity which is not dependent upon communication. One study found that the typical administrator spends about 75 per cent of his time communication and about 75 per cent of this time communicating in individual face-to-face situations. Too often, even though the parties are speaking the same language, understanding escape either one or the other. A few essential steps in the planning of communication are listed below:

1. Know your objectives. What is it that you intend to accomplish by this communication? The sharper the focus, the better the result.

2. Identify your audience. It is necessary to know who are you communicating with in order to select the proper language and the proper media.
3. Determine your medium (or media). The method of communication will often determine the success of the communication. A decision must be made on how best to communicate the message.
4. Tailor the communication to fit the relationship between sender and receiver. The key to this element of effective communication is the relationship climate. Is it one of fear or confidence?
5. Establish a mutuality of interest. Empathy, the ability to see the other person's point of view, is a priceless ingredient of effective communication.
6. Watch your timing. This is critical to the effectiveness of the communication. It is important to decide who should receive the communication first.
7. Measure results. Has the desired response occurred?

Essentials of Good Communication

It is a well-established principle that there is a positive relationship between good supervisory communication and effective performance. There are basic rules which are the cornerstones of successful communication:

1. Before communicating, clarify the idea in your mind. Too often we tend to communicate with undefined ideas and unclear objectives.
2. Examine the *real* objective of the communication. It is important to establish at the outset the goal or central reason for the communication.
3. Adapt the language of the communication and the setting to the specific situation. It is essential that the proper words be selected with regard to the intelligence and background of experience of the receiver. The total physical and human setting must be considered in planning for effective communications. This includes a sense of timing, and of course, the physical setting which must afford both participants privacy, if necessary.
4. It is often not what you communicate but how you communicate that will affect results. It is imperative that the sender be

sensitive to the importance of his tone of voice, expression and, of course, as mentioned before, his language.

5. Communications should be precise, brief and clear in presenting facts. Unnecessary words complicate communications. All facts should be stated in as objective terms as possible, avoiding abstractions and, whenever possible, providing illustrations.
6. Follow up communications. It is important to measure results to see how effective the communication was and, of course, learn from the mistakes of ineffective communicating.

Be a Good Listener

Sitting up and listening is half of the process of communication. Developing the art of listening requires relearning and unlearning bad habits developed over the years. Most of us do not know how to listen. We are often guilty of listening for facts or listening intelligently for the verbal statement alone when the art of listening is the discerning of ideas. Our biases also enter our listening habits. It is not unusual for certain words—rhetoric—to prejudice our appreciation and understanding. We may well not like the way a speaker "looks" or not like his voice and, therefore, pay little attention to, or discount what he has to say. Some of the prevalent and counterproductive listening habits follow:

1. Talking too much. It is obvious that if one talks too much, one cannot have enough time to listen:
   (a) Do you spend too much time explaining or defending your own position, thereby neglecting a careful evaluation of the other individual's position?
   (b) Are you so intent on framing the answer to a question which has yet to be fully communicated to you that you stop listening in the middle of someone's communication?
   (c) Are you often puzzled about what the other individual really meant?

   All of these actions require a reassessment of "talking" and "listening" habits. The key to these problems is in disciplining oneself to ask questions and wait—remaining silent—for enough time to pass for the other individual to communicate to you. It requires a disciplined approach to listening by appreciating the power of silence.

2. Asking leading questions. One of the most common pitfalls of communication is framing questions in such a way that the "right answer" is obtained:

   (a) Are you receiving only the answers you were secretly wishing for?
   (b) Are you receiving only limited responses which are guarded?

   In order to obtain the true responses of people to whom you are communicating, it would be best to outline the important areas in which questions should be asked and to frame the questions so that they are "open-ended". This will lead the other individual free to answer in any way and in as elaborate a fashion as he chooses.

3. Selecting the wrong time and the wrong place to communicate:

   (a) Is your communication hasty and does it reflect your desire to hurry it?
   (b) Do you have one foot out the door and only one ear unlocked when communicating?
   (c) Do you communicate in public when the subject cries for a private audience?
   (d) Are the phones ringing? Do people come and go freely in the middle of communication?
   (e) Do you communicate too soon or too late?

It is best to plan your communication time so that a full discussion can be had and the listener and speaker can give full attention to the discussion. It is also best to communicate in an atmosphere without distractions. It is important to be sensitive to the dignity of the listener; therefore, certain communications must be held in private and the listener should not be embarrassed in the presence of his peers.

Insulated Administrators

Many institutions have top administrators who are totally insulated from what is actually taking place in their own institution. It has been found that much of the information which reaches the chief executive is often incomplete and biased. This reflects a temperamental disposition on the part of the chief executive which filters down the line and makes obvious that he (the chief administrator) is not able to accept and

assimilate information which happens to conflict with his own values and predictions. There is a great deal of inaccuracy of information transmitted up the line. Add to this the many communication barriers and one would suspect a carefully designed attempt to filter information that reaches the chief administrator. There are many reasons for this:

1. No subordinate wishes to have his superior learn of anything he interprets to be actually or potentially discreditable to him. He, therefore, screens information and colours communication.
2. Subordinates soon learn what their supervisor desires to hear. The subordinate's personal anxieties, hostilities, aspirations and system of beliefs and values must inevitably shape and colour his interpretation and acceptance of what he has learned and is expected to transmit.
3. Subordinates are often desirous of impressing their superiors with the superiority of *their* contribution to the institution and, by the same token, of the inadequacies of the contribution of their rivals.

An administrator who wishes to obtain accurate information must develop an organizational style permeated by trust and confidence which will invite a free flow and exchange of information up and down the line.

Factors that Influence Meaning

How much and how accurately meaning is conveyed in communication depends on a number of factors which are listed as follows:

1. *The functional relationship between the sender and the receiver*—Very often they differ sharply in their policy thinking and their sense of values.
2. *The positional relationships between sender and receiver* —Is it that of an old-timer authoritatively instructing the newcomer? Is it that of a ruler speaking to one of his subjects?
3. *The group membership relationship*—Is it that of management speaking to management or a member of a union which is overtly hostile to management?
4. *Differences in heredity and prior environment*—Are the backgrounds of sender and receiver relatively the same? If not, meaning will be difficult to convey. Status in life powerfully shapes, ideas and attitudes.

5. *Differences in formal education*—What is the capacity of the audience to understand and comprehend the message?
6. *Past experience*—What has been the quality of the human relationships between sender and receiver?
7. *Emotions*—The current emotional state of the sender and receiver can determine whether the correct meaning is exchanged or whether all meaning will be blocked by an insurmountable barrier.
8. *Misunderstanding of words*—Words alone do not convey meaning. Only people can convey meaning through their use of words.

Communication has been compared to a radio set. First, you must select a station. The radio must be tuned for sending and the receiver must be tuned for reception. Selecting the station or the best wave length is critical. There are many messages involved in normal conversation, and often what the speaker means to say and what he actually says differ; in addition, what the other person hears is not always what the other person thinks he hears. In order to maximize communication skills and communicate what you intend to communicate, you should keep the following principles in mind:

1. Before sending a message, clarify your intentions.
2. In shaping your intentions into language or "code", be certain it is couched in a language or code that the receiver will be able to manage with facility.
3. In transmitting, make certain that all of the media which exist as a channel of communication between the sender and the receiver are being exploited so that the major portion of the message has a possibility of getting through to the receiver.
4. One of the basic requirements of good communication is that the sender have in mind an accurate image of the receiver.
5. This, of course, requires that he have an image of the receiver himself, his interests, endowments and attitudes toward the sender and the environment in which the message is taking place.
6. Good communications require that there be some interchange, back and forth, between the sender and the receiver in order that the normal, natural inconsistencies and lack of clarity between the sender and receiver in any message be made clear.

Communication Media

Institutions primarily make use of four methods of communication: meetings and conferences, departmental letters, written memoranda and bulletin boards.

Meetings and Conferences

Probably the most widely used method of communication is through meetings and conferences. A critical point in such vehicles is the ability for two-way communication. Conferences usually fall into a didactic pattern with all messages going one way. A conference that provides for discussion and encourages normal give-and-take can be most effective in the communication network. The truly effective conference involves a group of people pooling ideas and experiences. It is well to appreciate that the most effective conference develops from the acceptance of certain preconditions:

1. The meeting is called for a definite purpose, clearly understood by the chairman and participants.
2. The size of the group is limited.
3. Attention is given to the proper grouping of employee levels for the purpose clearly understood.
4. The conference is of a definite length, and time of starting and ending is invariable.
5. A conference room should be large enough and comfortable enough.
6. Advance materials should be distributed to avoid time-consuming activities while the conference is on.

Departmental Letters

Letters sent from institution or a department of the institution to employees are usually used in special circumstances. The announcement of long-range plans or of proposed changes are suitable subjects for such letters. To be successful they should be brief and careful attention directed to the language. This method is regarded as one of the most effective methods of communication. Such letters are also used to welcome new employees, announce changes in employee wage scales and fringe benefits, and in circumstances where the administrator or

departmental head wishes to address a general appreciation to all employees. The cardinal rule here is that the institution should use such letters only when they have something of the utmost importance to communicate. Letters are probably the most personal of the communication vehicles. Most experts would agree that style is as important as content. Brevity, simplicity and a straightforward approach are all attributes of sound written communications. Careful attention should be directed toward common errors in written communications.

Written Memoranda

Included in this category are the memoranda used between departments, between executives and between levels of employees. This form of communication has the advantage of permanence and verifiableness. It is often used to ensure follow-through between levels of supervision. The largest single criticism of this form of communication is that of wasted time and material: messages contained in memoranda can often be communicated, more effectively, by telephone or personal visits. It is well to keep in mind that the written memo loses the most important attributes of oral communications—intonation and facial expressions. Brevity should be observed in this form of communication. If action is required, such action should be clearly indicated along with the requested timing. Memoranda with hidden agenda are inappropriate. Directness and specificity are key ingredients of effective written memoranda. It is best to keep a copy of a memorandum that you have initiated, and good practice to send copies of your memoranda to any individual mentioned therein who may be affected by what you have communicated.

Bulletin Boards

Bulletin boards are an effective communication vehicles for formal announcements. They are most effective when they are able to attract employees by constant changes and careful control of content including prompt removal of out-of-date material. To obtain maximum efficiency from the use of bulletin boards, they should be placed near an entrance or exit, in staff common rooms or outside the administrator's office. Most institutions that make excellent use of bulletin boards agree that each department should have its own bulletin board. Two-section boards have been found to be the most efficient. One side is used for routine notices of the department while the other section is used for news items, special

features, posters and general announcements of a personal nature. The use of posters is an effective and attractive way of getting the institution's message across. Posters may be used in formal series. Here again, constant change is necessary to keep the employee's attention. It is well to date all notices, first with the posting date and second for the removal.

Policy and Employee Manuals

An essential ingredient of a total communication network is the preparation and distribution of a personnel policy manual and an employee manual. Sound personnel administration encourages and facilitates the employee's optimum contribution toward an understanding of the objectives of the institution. The purpose of the personnel policy manual is to provide administrative and supervisory staff members with a complete documentary on the institution's personnel administration so that the policies and procedures approved by the institution's board may be applied equitably, consistently and with authority. Personnel policies should be designed to promote the mutual understanding, respect and cooperation necessary to maximize the delivery of services in the institution. The institution must develop specific policies in the areas of employment, placement, promotions, compensation, benefits, training, disciplining, labour relations and many other facets of personnel administration.

Policy is a guide to action against which the administrator and the supervisor can measure their immediate, routine decisions that are often made under time pressure. Personnel policy is a simplification and logic-bringing instrument which assists in problem solving and decision-making.

The employee handbook is an offshoot of the personnel policy and procedure manual. It is more informal than its parents. Its intent is to explain as clearly as possible the policies and rules, and general information of the institution. Many employee manuals are broken down into sections. The manual starts off with a welcome letter from the institution's chief executive. A section, "getting started", includes the organization's selection policies and deals with such varied subjects, necessary for proper induction of the new employee, as explanation of the probationary period, employee identification system and hours of work. Another section deals with compensation: how employees are paid, shift differentials, overtime practices and time records. Still another deals with important elements of "on-the-job" seniority, promotions, transfers and grievance procedures. A section, often quite large, will be set aside

for time off. This will include an explanation of the institution's policies on holidays, vacations, sick leave, etc. The fringe benefit programme is explained in another section. The obligations of the employee will be included in a separate section covering rules, regulations and general guidelines for cooperation. Employee manual are often illustrated. Every attempt should be made to make them readable and understandable.

SUMMARY

Communication is the focal point in a sound employee relations programme. Studies in human behaviour indicate a clear and urgent need for employees to know what is expected of them and where they stand in the organization. The development of formal communication programmes is critical to successful administration. Too often, top administration makes decisions which are autocratically imposed upon the rest of the organization. Without appropriate participation and maximum communication, an organization may well fall below its expected goals. The hallmark of a sound communication programme in an institution is the development and distribution of a personnel policy manual. Policies, plans and goals should be developed and communicated through various vehicles: conferences, meetings, face-to-face discussions. An organization that develops an atmosphere which facilitates and encourages upward and downward communication will ensure its own success. Communication is not the responsibility of only a few people. Every member of the management team must be a good communicator. The supervisor's chief responsibility is getting the work done through other people. In order to accomplish this, a supervisor must be trained in the art of communication which also includes an appreciation of the importance of listening as an integral part of the entire process.

HANDLING PROBLEMS, COMPLAINTS AND GRIEVANCES

The solving of institution's problems and effective handling of employee complaints and grievances affords the supervisor or administrator the greatest opportunity to win over employee respect and gain their confidence. The most important employer-employee relationship is the one that exists between the worker and his or her immediate supervisor. It is essential for supervisors and administrators to know their people, be genuinely interested in them, and recognize their needs and problems. This good relationship cannot only head off many problems before

they reach the formal grievances stage, but also lead to increased productivity.

The supervisor is often the day-to-day interpreter of institutional policy, rules, and regulations and the administrator of the union contract, if there is any. If there is a Pandora's box in the day-to-day employer-employee relationship, it is the area of grievances. An unattended accumulation of minor irritations and aggravations may inflate and finally explode in the supervisor's face. A little bit of attention at the beginning will go further than a great deal of harried and pressured attention at the end. As a matter of fact, most complaints can be satisfactorily resolved by the supervisor before they become final grievances.

A grievance may have some basis in fact or it may be fabricated or exaggerated beyond reality. A grievance may not truly be a grievance in the classical sense. More often than not, it may be a gripe or just information-seeking on the part of the employee. In any case it must be dealt with and resolved.

Minimizing Grievances

Although there is no way to completely eliminate grievances, there are commonsense guidelines that will reduce the number and the cost of grievances. Here are some suggestions:

1. Be alert for common causes of irritation within your department. Correct minor irritations promptly before they explode into major problems.
2. Do not knowing violate established policy, procedure, or practice. This, of course, requires the supervisor to be completely familiar with all policies and contractual clauses that affect the supervisor-employer relationship.
3. Keep promises. Do not make commitments you cannot keep. Many grievances are over the non-fulfillment of a commitment made by a supervisor.
4. Let your employees know how they are getting along. Don't wait for the formal performance review to keep an employee informed of progress or problems. This will minimize the number of grievances that develop when employees are warned about poor performance after having received positive performance reviews earlier in the year.
5. If an employee doesn't measure up, let that employee know.

Find out why there is a problem and provide direction and coaching.

6. Encourage constructive suggestions: act on these suggestions where feasible and give proper recognition to the originators. Participation will go a long way to minimize grievances that may develop because of policy changes.
7. Assign and schedule work impartially: avoid favouritism in respect to working conditions or employee benefits.
8. Be sure your employees understand the meaning of and reasons for your orders and instructions. Use language that is meaningful from their point of view.
9. Be consistent in your words and actions unless there are important reasons for deviation. Where deviation is justified, clearly communicate those reasons to the employees. Explain changes in or deviations from policy, procedure or established practice.
10. Act promptly on reasonable requests from your employees. Don't keep employees waiting for answers to their questions. Nothing is more destructive than a grievance allowed to grow because of lack of prompt response on the part of the supervisor. Remember, you may have to say "no", but a constructive and sympathetic "no" can do less damage than a harsh "yes".
11. If corrective action must be taken, take it promptly; but do not discipline an employee in public.

Hearing a Complaint

Many gripes are not *bona fide* grievance because they concern situations not specifically covered by an institutional policy. Although a gripe may not qualify as a grievance, the employee should be heard on the subject. If a legalistic attitude is assumed at this stage and the gripes are dismissed summarily, hard feelings will be engendered and another issue properly subject to the grievance machinery will be used to exert pressure. It is not suggested that every petty gripe be given undue importance. However, the employee should not be brushed off without having the complaint fully heard.

Hearing a complaint requires attentive listening—get the complete facts and the underlying attitudes and feelings. Let the employee talk without interruption. Then ask questions until you are satisfied that you understand the specifics of the complaint and the true agenda. Do not

become predisposed or argumentative in response to the employee's answers. Very often, complaints reflect dissatisfaction in areas other than those under discussion. It is essential that you find out what is really bothering the employee. An excellent approach is to rephrase the employee's statement in your own words. This "reflection" serves four important purposes:

1. The employee is able to correct any misunderstanding you may have.
2. The employee has the opportunity to bring the complaint into closer focus.
3. You and the employee can assume that you understand the situation thoroughly.
4. The employee is assured that both of you are "on the same wave length", that you are empathetic and trying to understand the problem from the employee's point of view.

Further explanation or discussion should be reserved until after the facts have been checked, applicable policies reviewed and past practices, grievances, and commitments analyzed. Don't promise anything at this time other than a careful investigation. Specify a time within which an answer will be forthcoming. Don't mislead the employee by promising to do something about the complaint unless you are sure remedial action is in order.

There may be instances where a quick response is indicated. If you are absolutely certain of the facts, an immediate reply is in order. However, in most instances a hasty decision can be disastrous. If you are not sure of the facts, not sure of the appropriate policy provision, or doubtful that the emotional climate is conducive to resolution, delay your response.

Getting the Facts

After hearing and understanding the complaint, initiate an investigation. A complete investigation includes interviewing other employees who may have been involved, reviewing relevant records, and in general "stepping back" from the problem to gain objectivity. New facts and additional viewpoints are almost always uncovered in this way.

In your investigation, look for information concerning previous settlements of similar problems and relevant policy interpretations. You may call on other supervisors or department heads. Precedent becomes very important. A hasty decision may provide a precedent with far-reaching impact. Many a supervisor has found that a hasty or careless

decision over a relativity minor occurrence becomes important later in a different situation with more serious consequences. It is, therefore, essential that you investigate before you act.

Decision-making Time

After analyzing all the facts uncovered by a thorough investigation, it is time to develop a solution to the problem and an answer to the complaint. It is a good idea to discuss your proposed solution with others. Checking out your hunch, your conclusion or your suggested options with others who are in a position to assess their probable impact is a good idea. Ask your supervisor, or other department heads. Ask how this type of problem has been handled in the past. Consultation is a sign of caution, not indecision. You will not be criticized for reviewing your options with others if you have assembled the facts carefully and approached the grievance objectively.

Now it is time to put your answer in written form. Wherever possible, completely explain the reasons behind your decision. It is important that you deal with the specific complaint and not go beyond that complaint.

Communicating to the Employee

Supervisors who admit to their mistakes are more respected than those who cover up mistakes. If a grievance has merit and an error has been made, admit this to the employee and indicate your intention to take immediate corrective action. Make certain that you take such corrective action.

If the complaint has no merit and the grievance is to be denied, a full explanation should be communicated to the employee. Attempt to gain the employee's understanding and acceptance of your decision. If the employee remains dissatisfied, don't get impatient and irritated. Appeals are normally provided for in institutional grievance procedures, and the procedure for such an appeal should be explained to the employee. Finally, a written record of all that occurred should be kept in the departmental files.

General Guidelines

The following points on effective problem solving and grievance

handling are important for the supervisor to review and accept:

1. There should be a strong desire to resolve dissatisfaction and conflicts before they become real problems.
2. Supervisors should empathize with their employees, try to understand employee problems, and be able and willing to listen in a non-judgmental fashion.
3. The supervisor should have a sound working knowledge of personnel policy procedure and, if needed, the union contract.
4. The supervisor must balance a personal commitment to the interests of the institution with a sense of fair play on behalf of the employees. The supervisor represents the employees to the administration and the administration to the employees. Generally speaking, the supervisor's responsibility in grievance procedures embraces four primary functions:
   (i) Investigating the material facts,
   (ii) Analyzing the grievance to determine its basic causes,
   (iii) Discussing and answering the grievance, and
   (iv) taking action to eliminate present problems and prevent future ones.

If you are to discharge your responsibilities properly, your first task upon receiving a grievance is to investigate, not evaluate.

Here are some of the ways to improve human relations when handling problems, complaints and grievances:

1. *Be available*—Know your people are individuals and fit your methods to the individual. Cool off the hothead with patience: sense when something is troubling the quiet worker who keeps anger bottled up until it explodes; calm the sensitive employee who may think he or she is being slighted. You can't solve the problems of strangers, and unless you are approachable, you will have strangers working for you.
2. *Be relaxed*—When employees bring you gripes, real or fancied, let them sound off. If they see you are listening and will give them a fair hearing, the complaint won't look so big.
3. *Get the facts*—Get the story and get it straight. Ask questions to straighten out inconsistencies. Be objective and sympathetic.
4. *Investigate carefully*—Never accept hearsay. Find out for yourself the answers to such questions as who, what, when,

where and why. Check how the institutional policy covers the alleged offense, and review your files for precedence.

5. *Be tactful*—Many employees will start to tell a supervisor about unfair treatment only to realize halfway through their story that they don't have a real complaint. If the supervisor helps such employees "save face", he makes a friend. You never want a worker to leave the grievance interview humiliated and embarrassed.
6. *Act with deliberation*—Snap judgment leads to impulsive action. Take time to get all the facts. What caused the grievance? Where did it happen? Has an institution policy been violated? Has the employee been unfairly treated? Has there been favouritism, unintentional or deliberate? Was this grievance related to others?
7. *Get the answer*—May be it is impossible to solve the problem immediately, but don't give employees the runaround. If you can't get the facts you need to settle this case, say so. If the employee knows you are working on the problem, he or she is likely to be more reasonable.
8. *Consider the consequences of your decision*—Make sure you know the effect your settlement will have, not only on the individual, but on the group.
9. *Admit mistakes*—You are human and make mistakes, so if your decisions are occasionally reversed by higher-ups, admit your error. Don't bear a grudge against the employee who was proved right at your expense.
10. *Sell your decision*—When you deny an employee's grievance, explain why? A blunt "no" causes resentment. Don't pass the buck by blaming your denial on higher management. Supervision means leadership.

Research indicates that upper management depends significantly on the first-line supervisor to solve problems. Yet supervisors seem not to give high priority to this important responsibility. This would lead us to believe that supervisors do not fully realize that their role is fundamental in minimizing grievances and preventing a complaint from becoming a major dispute. Research data also indicate that the resolution of grievance process leads to more harmonious labour-management relationships. The first-line supervisor is key to that improvement.

SUMMARY

1. Employees deserve a complete and empathetic hearing of all complaints and grievances they present.
2. The most important job in the handling of problems is getting at the facts. Therefore, listen attentively, encourage a full discussion and defer judgment.
3. Look for the hidden agenda. Look beyond the selected incident; judge the complaint in context.
4. While you are investigating the problem, try to separate fact from opinion or impressions. Consult others when appropriate.
5. After you have come to your decision, promptly communicate that decision to the employee.
6. Written records are most important, they serve as a review for the supervisor to ensure consistency.
7. Follow-up is essential. Even if the employee does not appeal your decision, you should check back to see if the decision "took" or was upheld. There is no better way to win employee respect than to give due recognition to employee problems. A little way of follow-up goes a long way.

ASSESSING EMPLOYEE PERFORMANCE

It is an essential duty of an administrator to evaluate the performance of his subordinates at the end of the probationary period, and at least once every year. The evaluation must be made in writing and discussed with the employee. Each performance review form is made a part of the employee's permanent employment record.

In considering employees for promotions or annual salary increases, administrators should evaluate many factors such as teaching skill, knowledge, seniority, dependability and interest in the work. Performance reviews play a decisive role in increasing career opportunities at the institution.

It does not matter at which organization level an employee is: he wants to know where he has been, where he is now and where he is going. Every member of an organization wants to know exactly what the organization and, specifically, his boss expect him to do; how his performance will be measured; what his boss thinks of him; which areas need improvement; and how to move up in the organization. It is the responsibility of the administrator to fulfill this need.

It is immaterial how well-adjusted an administrator is: almost all abhor the necessity to criticize a subordinate's work. Not only is it easier not to say anything, it is (paradoxically) even easier to terminate a subordinate's employment than to do the distasteful work of improving his performance. Although most people agree with the general concept and purpose of formal employee performance appraisal programmes, some express reservations regarding their usefulness and benefits. In some instances personal experience has caused people to doubt the validity of such programmes. In other instances developing and implementing employee performance appraisal programmes has resulted in disappointment. Unfortunately, these misgivings are used all too often as justification for total inaction in a personnel programme that could help improve employee productivity, job satisfaction, compensation, stability and morale. A properly planned, developed, and implemented employee performance appraisal programme should preclude the possibility of failure and should prove most beneficial as a tool by which management can motivate its employees.

Much of the controversy surrounding the evaluation process springs from the justification or lack of justification for the programme. The key question here is: What will the programme accomplish? There is little difference of opinion on the fact that with or without a formal programme, administration will analyse and always has analyzed the performance of its employees. The appraisal function is a fundamental human act. The supervisor who obtains the best from his employees is the one who creates the best atmosphere or climate of approval within which his work group operates. He accomplishes this through the following methods:

1. He develops performance standards for his employees and sets them high to stretch the employees.
2. He measures performance against these standards.
3. He constantly commends above-par performance.
4. He always lets employees know when they have performed below par.

It is clear from this description that the essential justification for employee assessment is *achievement*, personal and institutional. It is essential that every supervisor should appraise his subordinates periodically and communicate his evaluation.

What is Performance Assessment?

Performance assessment is a method of evaluating an employee's work

performance on the job to which he is assigned. Other names for this method include merit rating, employee evaluation, performance review, performance rating, efficiency rating, personnel progress report, employee rating and man rating. Whenever these names occur, they all mean the same thing: evaluating the employee's work performance. *Job evaluation* seeks to rate the value of the job with no regard to the performer; conversely, *performance assessment* or *merit rating* rates the person who actually performs the job.

Why Performance Assessment?

The assessment of employee performance is an essential management tool in evaluating employees for purposes of promotion, transfer, training needs and wage determination; in addition, it functions as a communication vehicle to bolster employee motivation and reduce counter-productive differences in conception of duties, priorities, and accomplishment between the superior and the subordinate. Some administrators consider the employee performance review as a once-a-year administrative chore—a routine obligation that must be discharged in order to satisfy the school board, personnel department, or higher management. They consider the completion of the review form a tedious task and the conduct of the interview a superficial personnel ritual. Indeed, they find the communication of the assessment embarrassing, distressing, and without any redeeming virtues. More enlightened administrators view the assessment process as a golden opportunity to reinforce their relationship with the staff. They see it as a mechanism to provide support and guidance to the employee to ensure improved performance and development.

The primary purpose of the performance assessment is to *help the employee improve his performance by:*

1. Developing and obtaining acceptance by the employee of the specific standards against which his performance will be measured.
2. Evaluating the employee's performance in terms of these standards.
3. Developing and following a plan of action to help him overcome obstacles to his development and to strengthen his capabilities.
4. Soliciting the reactions, resolving differences and reaching a mutual understanding of the implications of the review.

5. Offering constructive suggestions and tangible assistance to the employee toward his development.

In the final analysis, the question of whether an institution shall or shall not rate the people who work for it is an academic one. An institution has no real choice in this matter. Administration *must* evaluate the performance of all employees. Judgments *must* be made and the only consideration is *how* to make them. Unquestionably, an appraisal programme can supply a yardstick to measure employees accurately. But who is to weigh the factors? Who, for instance, is to determine the factors that could accurately measure employee performance? It is the administrator's responsibility to develop such a yardstick in consultation with representatives of the line administration. A programme must be developed which will rate employees on the basis of an organized and systematic format which has as its cornerstone methodology incorporating common standards of judgment which can be applied uniformly by all raters. This is an essential ingredient since many performance assessment programmes fall short of their mark because the factors being rated are interpreted quite differently by the different raters. Standardization of terms is a key to the successful assessment programme.

Rating Systems

Performance assessment may be completed by one of several techniques.

1. *Assessment interview*— Here the supervisor meets with the employee and discusses the employee's performance, offering an opportunity for response.
2. *Rating scales*— These scales are the graphic or multiple steps which require checking of an appropriate point along a scale of value.
3. *Employee comparison systems*— These systems do not require the use of an absolute standard; rather the rater is asked to compare the individual employee with other employees being evaluated.
4. *Checklists*— This method provides an opportunity for the rater to indicate the employee's performance by entering checks in the various spaces provided.

The last three methods involve the use of a formal rating system and may be augmented by a personal interview between the rater and the rated after the assessment is made. The *Interview method* involves a face-to-face interview between the employee and the person rating him and is usually accompanied by a formal report of the discussion. The *Rating scale method* provides for the employee to be rated against some "standard" that is defined or otherwise described on a scale. It is the most widely used method. Typically these scales are made up of five or more traits or characteristics. The most common characteristics are productivity, quality, job knowledge, versatility, dependability, initiative, appearance, personal relations and cooperation with management. In selecting the traits to be included on a performance evaluation form, there are certain basic considerations. One should choose traits that are:

1. Specific rather than general.
2. Definable in terms to be understood by all raters.
3. Common to as many employees as possible.
4. Clearly distinguished from other traits.
5. Observable in the day-to-day performance of employees.

Some of the most common elements in a rating scale are defined as follows:

1. *Productivity*— (How much work is done consistently by the employee?) This element refers to the amount of productive work done by a given employee over a period of time. Depending on the nature of the job, the output can be measured by the number of research publications, or instructional devices produced, or it can be based on other measures (both good and bad) of quantity.
2. *Quality*— (How accurate, neat, or complete is the employee's work?) This element refers to the relative merit ("goodness" or "badness") of the employee's work. It refers to wastage; the effective use of supplies, equipment, and materials; and the meeting of specified acceptable standards. It should not be confused with job knowledge, which is concerned with understanding, nor with productivity, which refers to the quantity of production.
3. *Job knowledge*— (How well does the employee understand his job assignment?) This element refers to the employee's job

know-how. It refers to whether he has the necessary skills for his job and whether he can recognize defects in his work. It attempts to show if he knows how to meet the duties of his job, whether or not he acts accordingly.

4. *Versatility*—(Does the employee demonstrate ability to perform a variety of tasks?) This element refers to the mental and physical flexibility and adjustment necessary for satisfactory performance on a variety of jobs. It refers to the ability to change easily from one task to another.
5. *Dependability*—(How faithful is the employee in reporting to work and staying at his assigned work?) This element refers to the consistency with which an employee applies himself to his work, not to the amount of output or the quality of his work. It attempts to measure whether he works continuously. It refers to his attendance and punctuality; whether he remains at his job or wanders about; and whether he wastes time, loafs or works in spurts.
6. *Initiative*—(How well does the employee begin an assignment without directions?) This element refers to the employee's willingness and ability to initiate tasks; to recognize the best way of doing them; and to follow-up when necessary, with minimal supervision and direction.
7. *Appearance*—(Does the employee's personal appearance meets the standards for the job?) This element refers to the employee's personal grooming, attire, physical bearing and taste. An employee's attire usually is dictated by the nature of his work, which should be considered in evaluating this element.
8. *Personal relationships*—(How well does the employee relate to fellow employees?) This element refers to the general pattern of social conduct demonstrated by the employee at his job. It refers to how well he gets along with fellow employees and may be related to such diverse areas as health, alcohol, family and finances. Because this element represents a broad judgment of personality deviations from established norms, evaluators should rate it cautiously.
9. *Cooperation with management*—(Does the employee accept assignments and suggestions willingly?) This element refers to the employee's willingness to follow orders. It is related to his ability and desire to work with his supervisors as a team and to whether he resists or actively supports approved changes. It should not be confused with passive acceptance of orders or mere verbal "yessing" of supervisors to gain favour.

Frequently, words or phrases are placed at various locations underneath the line of a rating scale for each trait to indicate different degrees of the trait. From three to five "levels" of the trait are usually so characterized including the two at the extremes. Points are assigned to various degrees of each trait together with a total point range for the trait. By adding together the points that the employee receives on each trait, a single point value—a total score—is deduced.

In employee comparison systems of performance assessment, the relative performance of various employees in a group is compared one against another. In such man-to-man comparisons, individual characteristics, rather than the whole-man rating, are used. Each characteristic is described by five gradations. The high man and the low man are scored, and their names are put in appropriate positions on the scale. All other employees are compared with the names at the top and bottom of each trait to arrive at a rating.

In a modification of this method, the names of a group of employees known to several supervisors or department heads are listed on a form. Each head selects the one whose present performance he considers *highest* and the one he considers *lowest*. Then he continues down the list to select the *next highest, next lowest,* until all are rated. He selects alternately until all names listed have been ranked. No specific guide of factors to be considered is used. Each ranker makes his own definition of what will put one man higher or lower than others on the list.

Other types of employee comparison seeks to place all employees in a group in the order of relative performance, with best performance at the top and worst performance at the bottom. Some seek to force the distribution of any group of employees being rated into the lowest, 10 percent; the next lowest, 20 per cent; the middle, 40 per cent; the next, 20 per cent; and the highest, 10 per cent.

The check list type of rating offers a number of traits, and the rater merely checks the statements that best fit his assessment of the individual being rated. The list may be constructed with questions, statements, phrases or words which describe the manner in which an employee might perform on the job. The choice of statements is the key to the success of this plan; too often they are permeated with platitudes.

A variation of the check-list technique is the forced-choice performance rating. This method offers a series of blocks of two or more behaviour descriptions which appear to the rater to be approximately similar or equal in their level of favourableness or unfavourableness. Yet in studies conducted, certain replies are associated

with certain levels of performance. An example of a block of behaviour descriptions used for rating training skills follows:

1. Patient with slow learners.
2. Lectures with confidence.
3. Keeps interest and attention of class.
4. Acquaints classes with objectives for each lesson in advance.

A block of unfavourable items is :

1. Does not answer all questions to the satisfaction of students.
2. Does not use proper voice volume.
3. Supporting details are not relevant.

Experience has indicated that certain items can determine the difference between poor and good teachers while others have very little to do with the performance or relative success of the teacher.

Developing Personnel Assessment Procedure

The key to designing a merit rating system is an evaluation of organizational needs. The system must be tailor-made to meet the needs of the organization. The steps in establishing a merit rating system include:

1. The determination of the traits to be rated. Usually the institution's administrative group will select traits which are specifically related to performance on the job.
2. Traits must be carefully defined so that each individual delegated the responsibility of assessing performance understands their meaning.
3. The traits selected must be broken down into "degrees" or "levels", and each degree, in turn, must be carefully defined.
4. The traits and degrees within the traits must be weighted. This process assigns point values to each trait which reflects the influence of that trait on the rating as a whole. The point values for degrees within each trait are established similarly by determining the amount of points for each degree of the trait.
5. The actual conducting of the rating. The employee's immediate supervisor should be responsible for the assessment of the employee's performance. This assessment should be reviewed

by the department head and agreement arrived at between both levels of administration. Most successful assessment plans include the discussion of the rating with the employee once the assessment has been completed. Such assessment conferences include a frank discussion of the employee's accomplishments and weaknesses. The appraisal interview involves the interaction of two people, each with his own purpose, knowledge, view-points and attitudes. While these differences may be difficult to reconcile, a well managed assessment interview can help to determine goals and mutually acceptable standards. Both parties can then identify the problems that hinder achievement of their goals and arrive at workable solutions.

A constructive assessment interview is a very valuable management technique. It does, however, require the application of considerable skill, thought and effort. Workers want to know how they stand with their supervisors and it has been found that the whole assessment programme is fruitless without a face-to-face communication of results, expectations and plans for improvement.

Administrative Appraisal

The assessment of employee performance does not stop with the subordinate staff. Administrative appraisal is necessary to strengthen administrative performance by developing a clear-cut mutual agreement on work objectives, plans, and personal and institutional goals. Too often a discomforting situation develops by the absence of sharing the organization's total objectives by the chief executive with his immediate subordinates. Most institutions are using a three-phased administrative appraisal programme directed toward the final goal of sharing total objectives:

1. The personal appraisal.
2. The peer appraisal.
3. The management appraisal.

A personal appraisal form is given to the administrator whose performance is to be evaluated. The administrator is asked to outline his job, describing the objectives, responsibilities and duties of the position as he understands them. He is then asked to list the phases of

his work that he performs well and those he performs only adequately, and to make specific suggestions as to how he can improve. The narrative form of appraisal includes a statement on what he needs for improvement from his supervisor, from his fellow workers, from the organization and from himself. The executive is then asked to look back on the past year and describe what he considers were his chief accomplishments; to look for the future and describe the areas that he thinks he could profitably develop from the view-point of his personal goals and the institution's needs; and to list the changes he would suggest to accomplish such development.

Concurrently, the executive's boss has selected one or two of the executive's peers and asked them to measures the effectiveness of his performance—specifically to tell how well he functions regarding the needs of their department and how he strengthened or weakened their own efforts to perform effectively. They are asked to outline the executive's principal strengths and weaknesses. This peer appraisal is confidential and is shared only with the administrator's boss. It does not become part of the administrator's file.

Finally, after receiving the peer appraisal and the self appraisal forms, the administrator's boss or supervisor (from the management's side) is asked to complete a two-part appraisal form based on the assumption that performance improves with coaching and self-development.

The first part of the form lists various phases of the administrator's responsibility: professional knowledge, willingness to assume responsibility, planning, controlling work flow and expenditures, and accomplishment. Here the superior is asked to measure the administrator's problem-solving abilities, report writing, meeting of deadlines; his organizational development and relations with the staff; his staff development and communications with subordinates and superiors. In each of these categories the supervisor is asked to identify which of four statements presented to him most accurately reflects the administrator's actual performance and then to support each of his ratings by briefly setting forth instances during the past year that demonstrate the administrator's performance in these areas.

The second part asks the superior key questions about the administrator to be answered in narrative form. Among the questions are: What are his main strengths? In what respects is he least effective? What actions are you taking to help him improve his performance? Can you suggest any training or experience that will assist him in his

development? This form then serves as the basis of the appraisal interview which is conducted in complete privacy. The interview aims not at criticism, but at improvement of performance through recognition of an administrator's strengths and weaknesses.

Pitfalls of Rating

In making ratings there are several pitfalls which should be avoided:

1. Do not let your rating on one factor or your overall impression of the employee influence your rating of other factors.
2. Length of service or job classification should not affect the rating.
3. Do not let your personal bias enter into the rating.
4. Do not be swayed by previous ratings.
5. Do not rate on vague impressions.
6. Do not rate "sympathetically". If there are special circumstances, note them on appropriate catchall section of the form.
7. Do not hesitate to go on record with your true opinion.

Ratings, wherever possibie, should be made from accurate data or from observation. Ratings should not be based on employee performance during the entire period being reviewed. The rater should be careful not to emphasize recent happenings or isolated dramatic happenings which are not characteristic performances. If an employee has had more than one supervisor during the rating period, each superior should complete a separate rating form. A composite rating can then be determined by the present supervisor. In the assessment interview, it is imperative that it be conducted in private. The employee should be permitted to read the review form, and an explanation of the supervisor's appraisal of the employee in terms of the requirements of-the-job—not in terms of the personal characteristics of the employee—should follow. Where possible, references should be made to the position description or job outline. The employee's reactions should be solicited. The supervisor should listen attentively and actively. Criticism should be constructive and an emphasis placed on improvements to be made rather than on past failures. Unfavourable comparisons with other employees have no place in the assessment interview. If an employee's performance is deficient, it must be improved. He must be apprised of this fact. He must be told where he stands and agreement arrived at on future goals. The final step is the

summary of the appraisal including the employee's strengths, areas for improvement, plans for effecting such improvement, assistance available to him and mutual commitment to the goals to be achieved during the coming review period.

The performance evaluation of employees is practical and necessary to ensure understanding and to obtain optimal agreement between worker and supervisor on the goals of the institution and the progress (or lack thereof) of the employee in reaching institutional and personal goals. A typical evaluation plan will be conducted as follows:

1. Rate employees in your department on one factor at a time.
2. Select the employee who excels in this one factor and give your rating.
3. Select the employee who should receive the lowest rating on that factor, and give your rating.
4. Consider the remaining employees, one at a time, and by comparison (forced choice) with the highest and lowest rated employees, determine the proper rating.
5. After rating all employees in the group on one factor, follow the same procedure for each of the other factor.
6. After rating on all factors, review each form, taking into consideration the complete picture.
7. Ratings should be made from accurate data whenever possible, or from observation.
8. The rating should be based on the employee's performance during the entire period being reviewed. The rater should be careful not to overemphasize recent happenings which are not characteristic performances.

Some change must be legislated if it is to be both permanent and positive. To ensure purposeful change, employee understanding must be obtained. This understanding includes the discovery of things the employee will both like and dislike: if change is to be effected, the worker must learn about both.

DISCIPLINING OF EMPLOYEES

If you are a supervisor or administrator you are going to be faced, almost daily, with the need to effect corrective action when an employee is chronically late, has an absence problem, disregards a rule or policy of

the institution, refuses to follow an order, is unproductive, is uncooperative, or in some ways does not meet the standards of the institution. Taking corrective action is often a euphemism for discipline. On the other hand, the goal of positive discipline is to salvage the employee, to correct the behavioural pattern that is either anti-social or anti-institution.

More often than not, the act of disciplining is conceived of as punishment. Such an approach is referred to as negative discipline. We shall deal here with the complete spectrum of *constructive* discipline.

Good and Just Cause

There must be a "good and just" cause for a disciplinary action and the burden of providing it rests on administration. If cause has been proved, a penalty imposed by the administration will not be modified by an arbitrator, unless it is shown to have been clearly arbitrary, capricious, discriminatory, or excessive in relation to the offence. The key point to understand about limitation on the right to discipline is that administration may discipline up through discharge *only* for sufficient and appropriate reasons.

It behooves the administration to develop a sound procedure, based upon due process, for the discipline of employees. Even if it is not mandated by a collective bargaining agreement, due process should be available to all employees. Arbitrators will normally support a management action if progressive discipline includes, first, a verbal reprimand and full explanation of what is necessary to remedy the situation, followed by written reprimand for a second infraction and a clear warning of the future penalties that may be imposed. A final warning and suspension may follow, and subsequently the ultimate penalty of discharge.

The arbitrator will also consider whether or not the employee was fully aware of the standards against which his or her behaviour was measured. These standards include basic rules and regulations that outline offences which subject employees to disciplinary action, and the extent of such disciplinary action.

Disciplining has become more juristic and legalistic with the advent of a union, but that does not mean that it is impossible to discipline employees. It does mean that the administration must record actual events, offences and transgressions. You cannot simply wish away problem employees. Here are some noteworthy rules for corrective discipline:

1. Discipline to be meaningful must be corrective, not punitive.
2. When you discipline one, you discipline all.
3. Corrective discipline satisfies the rule of equality of treatment by enforcing equally among all employees established rules, safety practices, and responsibility on the job.
4. Just cause or any other comparable standard for justifying disciplinary action consists of three parts:
   (a) Did the employee breach the rule or commit the offence charged against him?
   (b) Did the employee's act or misconduct warrant corrective action or punishment?
   (c) Is the penalty just and appropriate to the act or offence as corrective punishment?
5. The burden of proof rests on the supervisor. He or she must justify each of three parts that make up the standard of just cause.

Forms of Discipline

The real purpose of discipline is to correct employees so that unacceptable behaviour does not recur. In addition, you wish to deter others from committing the same errors. We have learned a great deal about the need for progressive disciplinary action. Most of what we have learned has come from two sources—the behavioural scientists and arbitrators.

Arbitrators tell us what is required to sustain a discharge. For illustration purpose, the following list provides a few criteria for the sustaining of discharges:

1. The employer must prove that the alleged acts occurred and were of sufficient gravity to warrant termination.
2. The employer must show that the misconduct was not condoned, but the employee was specifically warned of the consequences through progressive discipline, such as written warnings and suspensions.
3. The evidence must show that the employee made no genuine effort to heed the warnings although the consequences of continued misconduct were known.
4. The employee cannot be singled out for disparate treatment for offences that do not subject others to similar discipline.
5. When a long service employee is involved, there must be sound

cause to believe that the event are not transitory, but form a consistent and recurrent pattern that is unlikely to change in the future.

The Oral Reprimand

It is clear that progressive disciplining usually starts with oral reprimands or oral warnings. The function is often handled in a counselling session. What is the purpose of the action? It should be to nip in the bud behaviour that is inappropriate to the work area. The necessary ingredients for a successful counselling encounter are complete privacy, a well planned agenda, enough time to arrive at agreement, and a positive attitude on the part of the supervisor.

In such sessions employees should receive a complete outline of the action in question. Details should not be spared, and dates and times and places should be communicated. The specific institution policy or rule in question should be enunciated. The specific documents wherein such rules are contained should be examined. The employee should be given complete freedom to answer the charge, explain his or her behaviour, admit or deny the action.

It is obvious that an effective counselling session will develop from the point that the employee agrees that the action occurred and was inappropriate. If such an agreement is reached, a plan to improve the employee's performance should be discussed. It is also important at this time to acknowledge the positive aspects of the employee's behaviour.

We must repeat that the supervisor who wishes to effect corrective disciplining should be more interested in changing an employee's behavioural patterns and attitudes than in reprimanding that employee. Here are some pointers for the supervisor interested in making criticism more constructive:

1. Don't reprimand a worker who is angry or excited. Wait until he or she has cooled down. Wait until you cool down, too.
2. Don't bawl out someone in front of other people. This is embarrassing and humiliating and is likely to do more harm than good.
3. Find out how the worker feels and thinks about the situation. If you want someone to do something differently, you first have to find out what she or he already knows.
4. When you criticize a person, it is much better to compare her

or his performance to department standards than to the performance of another employee. A person is more likely to feel resentful or insecure if she or he is compared unfavourably to a co-worker.

5. Most important, if you reprimand constructively, you must show a person how to improve his or her performance. You don't want to destroy an employee's self-confidence. You want to build up confidence by guiding the worker in the direction of a satisfactory performance.

The oral reprimand or warning interview is a useful way for the supervisor to establish a sound relationship with *all* employees—those who require such warnings and those who do not. Employees normally respect supervisors who apply the rules of the institution fairly. Although criticism is often a disturbing element, the need for constructive criticism can be fully appreciated by employees.

If the supervisor is to discipline firmly and wisely, it is essential that the administration fully supports him or her in those instances where institutional policy is being protected and carried out. It is equally important that the administration of the institution provides clear evidence that the supervisor will be backed up at crucial moments. This does not mean that there will never be a situation where the supervisor is overruled, but such incidences should not be based on political pressures, legal technicalities or sentimentality. The responsibility of meting out discipline is difficult enough without undercutting the first-line supervisor.

Before concluding our discussion on the oral reprimand or warning interview, it should be made clear that the oral reprimand is not appropriate or effective in the face of flagrant offences such as insubordination, embezzlement, violence or moral crimes. Such actions call for sharper responses—often termination.

Warning Notices

Overt flaunting of institutional rules and appropriate behaviour patterns is dealt with by the first-line supervisor either by means of a formal warning notice, suspension, or discharge—if, and only after, a formal warning interview has been held. (This action does not apply if the transgression is a major and flagrant one such as those mentioned under exceptions to the oral reprimand). Some examples of negative behaviour which may call for a written warning notice are:

— Insubordination or impertinence
— Unauthorized or chronic absenteeism
— Chronic lateness
— Loafing or sleeping
— Misrepresentation of records
— Drinking alcoholic beverages
— Dishonesty
— Fighting on the job
— Gambling

The warning notice should not come as a surprise to an employee. It is essentially the second step in the arsenal of weapons used to reverse a poor behavioural pattern. It is often preceded by the oral reprimand, but may directly follow a clear violation of institutional rules and regulations. In preparing the warning notice, the supervisor is again concerned with facts and not with subjective opinions.

The institution normally provides a form to be used for written warning notices. This form usually calls for a clear statement of the specific rule or policy that has been violated. The supervisor may have to refer to the personal policy manual containing the specific rule.

Following the reference point, the written warning notice should move toward a description of the act in question. Once again the supervisor is urged to be specific and complete. Dates, time, and where appropriate, witnesses should be included.

Now we come to the most important part of the warning notice—a statement to indicate that immediate satisfactory improvement must be shown and maintained unless further disciplinary action is to be taken. In many cases, this "immediate satisfactory improvement" can be outlined in detail. For example, suppose an employee has shown a pattern of absenteeism—let us say two or three days each month for the last six months (many of the days were Mondays, making long weekends possible). The supervisor will indicate that the employee's pattern of Monday absences is not acceptable, that the employee's attendance will be monitored over the next two, three, or four months to gauge improvement, and that if there is no improvement, the employee will be subject to suspension and possible termination.

The warning notice is presented to the employee in private. If possible, the employee should be asked to sign the warning notice, acknowledging receipt. More important than this acknowledgment of the warning form is

the employee's acknowledgment that the behaviour is inappropriate and the improvement is forthcoming.

Despite the discussion above, it is important to remember that the supervisor's cardinal responsibility in this procedure is to attempt a restructuring of the employee's behaviour: it is not the primary responsibility or objective to punish the employee.

One bit of advice is necessary before we explore the final two steps in the disciplinary arsenal of weapons—suspension and termination. There is no easy panacea that can be offered in the area of behaviour control. In a few cases oral reprimands or warning notice will never be enough. In still more cases suspensions may be counter-productive. The supervisor must keep in mind that constructive disciplining is a means of achieving the end product— a change in behaviour patterns.

Suspension

The suspension is not universally accepted as an effective way to correct behaviour patterns. Many employees find the suspension a respite from the stress of the work area. Some employees even enjoy being out on strike. For an employee with a chronic absentee record a suspension is certainly not the worst sort of punishment.

A one-day suspension can be as effective as a one-week suspension. The shock of the suspension will usually bring the employee to his or her senses. The length of the suspension has little effect on the probability of rehabilitation. Very often the suspension of an employee causes inordinate difficulties in maintaining teaching schedules. I have come to the conclusion that a one-or two-day suspension is a sufficient final warning to employees before termination. The suspension should be accompanied with a written warning notice indicating prior attempts, both informal and formal, toward rehabilitation. Most important, the suspension should indicate that it constitutes the final warning.

Termination

In order to sustain a discharge where an arbitration procedure is available, the following minimal requirements must be met. In fact, these requirements should be operative whether or not there is an arbitration procedure, whether or not there is a union.

1. Facts must be presented, clearly indicating that the employee actually committed the offence. Opinions must be separated from hard documentation. Witnesses may be essential.
2. You must be able to display a consistent approach to the offence in question: no playing of favourites.
3. The record should indicate a progressive disciplining ladder, except in the case of blatant and serious offences.
4. The punishment must fit the crime.

Progressive disciplining normally must precede the discharge of an employee. The procedure for progressive discipline as outlined above includes a verbal reprimand and a full explanation of what is necessary to remedy the situation. Normally a second infraction calls for a written reprimand with a clear warning of future penalties which may be imposed. A suspension may follow with a final warning and the ultimate penalty is discharge.

Disciplining for Optimum Results

Should discipline be strict and severe or tolerant and easy going? The answer will not be found by locating the optimum point between strict and easy, but rather in the fundamental nature of the social organization which the supervisor must understand as part of his disciplining duties. If the basic mores of an organization are developed in a manner that commands the respect and conformance of its members, disciplining should offer no special problem. The rank and file member will observe the mores either automatically or because of the pressures exerted to do so by other members of the group. That is, he probably will if he has a feeling of belonging and thus recognizing that to belong requires a contribution in accordance with his means and talents. Thus, in essence, the supervisor's attempts to discipline must see discipline as a means not of immediately stopping an undesirable behaviour only, but of reaching a goal of desirable citizenship.

SUMMARY

1. Your primary concern in disciplining employees is to salvage them, *not* to scrap them.
2. Although punishment is part of disciplinary action, it is not the primary part.

3. Direct your attention, and therefore your plan of action, toward correcting improper employee actions.
4. Don't play favourites; be consistent; the rule of equality of treatment should pervade all your disciplinary actions.
5. *Just cause* must be established for all disciplinary action.
6. The punishment must fit the crime.
7. Progressive disciplining includes oral reprimands (including counselling), written warnings, suspension, and termination.
8. Self discipline develops where employees trust their supervisors and administrators, where they feel secure, and where they feel that they belong.

COPING WITH UNIONS

Whether he likes it or not, sooner or later, the school administrator will have to confront one or the other union that all institutions have in modern times. It may be in the form of a students' union, teachers' union, administrative staff's organization, or maintenance employee's negotiating force. Almost invariably, it is the principal of the institution who would be facing these unions as the first line of defence. It should also be emphasized at the same time that no one else can cope with the situation as well as he can.

Root Cause of Union-related Unrest

What upper management does or doesn't do, what labour lawyers retained as consultants for institutions do or do not recommend, what the board of trustees believes should be the basic philosophy of the institution—all of these are not as significant as the effect of the first-line supervisor on employees' desire or lack of desire to take collective action. More employees vote for or against their immediate supervisor than vote for or against the top administration, the board of trustees, or consultants. It is at the day-to-day level of intercourse between the first-line supervisor and the employees that the institutional life-style impacts upon the rank-and-file employee; that impact is critical in a union organizing campaign. Unions rarely organize employees; rather it is the administration's poor employee relations record (uppermost in that grouping is the first-line supervisor) that drives employees into unions.

Management failure is the root cause of the majority of successful union campaigns. Management failures can include a lack of

understanding of employee needs; a lack of competitiveness of salaries and fringe benefits; a lack of clear and usable communication lines; a lack of sound personnel policies; a lack of a formal and understandable grievance mechanism; a lack of appropriate and acceptable working conditions; the presence of arrogant, insensitive, overworked and harried supervisors.

It is also patently clear that institutions that provide all the benefits and conditions of a union shop—with all the protection inherent in a union contract, such as seniority provisions, grievance and arbitration mechanisms, promotional opportunities—will not become unionized. It is the absence of these conditions plus the presence of insensitive management that drives employees into unions.

Reasons for Employees Joining Unions

There is a myth that outside rabble-rousers, militants and politicians—often corrupt or radical in their politics, are responsible for organizing of employees. Experience, however, has shown that it may not always be so.

The decision to join is by no means strictly a natural decision. It is probably more like a religious conversion than like deciding to buy a pair of shoes. The worker does not estimate whether the results he will get from the union will be worth the dues he pays. He is confronted with an emotional appeal and urged to take part in a social and political crusade and he finally decides to accept. Moreover, the decision to join is usually not an individualistic decision. The first few workers who join the union have to make up their own minds. After a nucleus has been secured, however, the growth of the union develops into a mass movement. Most of the workers join because others have done so and hold-outs are gradually brought into line by the pressure of social ostracism.

We often look at unions as a movement. The fact is that most union members do not view the union as a movement, but rather as a means to an end—as a limited purpose economic institution. What they are looking for is what they cannot presently find in the institution. It is a matter of unfulfilled needs.

There is a marked relationship between worker morale and how much employees feel their boss is interested in discussing work problems with the work group. When the supervisor treats subordinates as human beings, there is greater group loyalty and pride. Employees with group loyalties and pride do not need unions to fill their needs. By seeing

problems through the eyes of the workers, the supervisor can translate employee needs to top management and thereby help arrive at policy decisions that are realistic and satisfy both administration and employees. Policies arrived at in this way will not drive employees into the arms of union organizers. It is a fact that the basic employee desires are for "full appreciation of work done", "feeling in on things", and "sympathetic help on personal problems". When an employee does not feel appreciated, is not in on things (does not know what is going on and most important, does not know about the things that affect his daily work life), or cannot look to his supervisor for empathy, then that employee will look elsewhere. The union stands ready to listen, to promise, to take up the battle for unfulfilled employee needs.

Some of the major dissatisfiers in the work area are: institute policy, administration, supervision, salary, inter-personal relations and working conditions. Similarly, some of the major satisfiers are: what the employee does, recognition, responsibility, advancement and achievement. By improving managerial practices and by proper utilization of both people and technology, the supervisor can increase the satisfaction and productivity of employees. Satisfied and fulfilled employees are not receptive to union organizers.

The Union Leader

The typical union leader has a natural affinity for people, is a good listener, and knows how and at what level to communicate. Here is a profile of a good union organizer.

(i) He or she has a natural capacity to like people. A union organizer is a warm, gentle, outgoing person who communicates well and relates effectively to all types of people.
(ii) He or she has the ability to adapt to the immediate surroundings and warm up to people very quickly.
(iii) He or she is patient with people. The union leader recognizes that non-union employees are not immediately sold on organization. Therefore, the leader makes an ongoing effort to sign up or convince all employees of the values of unionism and collective action.
(iv) Many labour relations experts have depicted organizers as a combination missionary, sales-person, psychologist.

In addition, a good union leader knows how to approach people. He no longer talks simply about wages and benefits. He establishes rapport with the workers on a much higher level. He knows when to raise the key issue of employee rights. He shows workers how to establish their rights, how to meet with management as equals, how to protect themselves as individuals, and how to win identity with the institution as important human beings.

Furthermore, the leader has two immediate objectives when he makes his first contacts with the workers at an institution. He is looking for leadership for his campaign and information about the specific problems and complaints of the employees.

There is no blueprint for meeting individual workers and gaining their confidence—conversations can be started in restaurants and street-corners, through leads passed on by other union members, and by acquaintances made through social affairs. If there is any rule at all, it is that contacts are *not* made by suddenly appearing at a school gate with a leaflet urging employees to sign a union authorization card right on the spot.

Most union organizers are interested primarily meeting the type of employee who is respected by his fellow workers and who has influence inside the institution. Getting to know a few of these employees is more important—at this stage—than meeting the maximum number of workers.

Once a potential leader has been contacted, it is important to win his confidence and trust. Time spent in developing this leader, answering his questions about the union, and explaining the benefits of collective bargaining will be well worthwhile after the organizing campaign gets under way and this leader becomes a union spokesman inside the target institution.

Articulate and respected leaders inside the organization are vital to any campaign, but the chosen representatives uses his own judgment in selecting the right people. He is always sure that they are not known as chronic "gripers' or "soreheads" and that they are not motivated simply by a desire for revenge or a driving personal ambition.

In the *perfect* campaign, the organizer will find a leader for every group in the organization—a woman for the female workers, leaders within minority, racial, and regional groupings, and spokesmen for the various departments and shifts. Since the *perfect* situation rarely exists, the staff man develops a leadership group as representative as possible.

Rating of Administrators by Employees

There is no question that the principal or the first-line administrator is the person most dramatically affected by the organization of employees. The institution itself may be exposed over the years to restrictions on management rights, increased wages, and increased fringe benefits, but in the final analysis the real impact of unionization is felt at the day-to-day level of supervisor employee intercourse.

The first-line administrator must understand the key role he or she plays during the organizational drive. The union is keenly interested in and often extremely aware of the day-to-day administrator-employee relationship, especially the issues of fairness and consistency. If the employees believe that they are not being treated fairly by their administrator, they will be more interested in the union's carefully presented approach in the area of employee rights. If the administrator has played favourites— has handled similar cases in different ways for different employees—then that administrator and that institution are more vulnerable to the organizer's demand for collective power to enforce such consistency and fairness. Employees look carefully at their administrator's behaviour in similar situations, looking for consistency in more cases than looking for the actual punishment. As we already know, a sympathetic "no" may be more effective than a harsh "yes". Similarly, a sympathetic "no" in one situation will be compared to the "yes" of the prior situation for the test of consistency. If your decision has been different in what may appear to be similar cases, it is important that you make the difference acceptable by sharing the underlying facts of both situations. But beware: if the underlying facts are similar and you still have reached a different decision, you must explain your reasons.

When groups of employees are faced with the choice of voting for or against the union, they often think in terms of their relationship to their supervisors. Critical to that relationship is a supervisor's integrity. How you are perceived by your employees when they are in the voting booth is a reflection of your actions over the years. Have you truly represented the workers to the management and the management to the workers?

Several suggestions that can produce group loyalty and high productivity (and most important, reflect favourably on your integrity) should be reviewed at this time:

1. Keep employees informed about developments.
2. Recommend pay increases where they are indicated.

3. Keep your people posted on how well they are doing.
4. Take the time to listen, empathetically, to employee complaints and grievances.
5. Permit employees to discuss work problems with you.
6. Recommend employees for promotional opportunities.
7. Don't take all the credit; share the product of your institution's labour with all participating and productive members of the team.
8. Display consistent and dependable behaviour.
9. Discipline in private.
10. Treat all members of your institution as equals.

Labour unions capitalize on management mistakes. The need for unionization is created by the management rather than the union. If the management (and that includes the first-line supervisor) does not understand and care about employee needs, the union wins the election. It is evident that institutions and supervisors have become increasingly sophisticated and aware of what drives employees into unions.

Knowing the Labour Laws

It is a common fact that whenever legal service or expert assistance is required, the services of a competent professional should be sought. There is no question that when a union approaches an institution that institution should have sound labour relations and, if necessary, legal advice. But in the final analysis a simple dose of common sense would suffice.

You, the first-line supervisor, will be on the firing line in such a situation. You will have to know what is and what is not permissible as far as the National Labour Laws are concerned. But given the pressures of the moment and the supervisor-employee relationships that have developed over the years in your institution, it may seem strange to deal with legalities at such a time.

Let's refer then to the overall common sense approach that has been complicated by legal interpretations. There are three basic prescriptions when dealing with employees during a union organizing campaign:

1. Don't threaten them.
2. Don't promise them any reward for staying out of the union.
3. Don't interrogate them, especially about their preferences. Never ask, "Are you for the union or are you against the union?"

Usually the labour laws state that you may not threaten employees with the loss of their jobs or reduction in their wages; you may not use threatening or intimidating language. Of course, even common sense directs you not to threaten employees in the exercise of their right to support a union.

Although you cannot personally urge an employee to convince other workers to oppose the union, you may tell employees that when a union enters an institution, problems about direct communication may arise, eliminating the one-to-one discussion between employee and the supervisor. You can share with employees the disadvantages of belonging to a union: paying dues and initiation fees, the possibility of loss of income due to strikes, the necessity for picket line duty. Without using threatening language, you may tell employees that the administration does not want a union and that the institution does not need a union.

You cannot promise increased wages, promotions, or benefits if employees reject the union. You can tell the employee that a union will out-promise an employer, but in the final analysis, the union cannot guarantee anything. It must bargain with the employer, and in order to attain benefit levels, must reach agreement with the employer. You may remind employees of their present benefits and compare these benefits with those in unionized institutions.

Supervisors may not ask employees their personal opinions about the union or what they believe are the feelings of other employees. You cannot call employees away from their work areas into your office to urge them to vote against the union. You cannot systematically visit the homes of employees to urge them to vote against the union.

You, as a supervisor, can tell employees that they do not have to sign union authorization cards, and indeed, do not have to speak to union organizers at their homes if they do not so desire. You can speak to employees individually or in groups at the employees' work station, in the employee common-rooms or in other areas where employees are accustomed to being. Remember, it is illegal to ask employees what they think about a union, or how they intend to vote, or if they have signed cards or attended union meetings. But it is permissible for you to tell employees why a union is not necessary in your institution. You may continue to operate normally and continue to discipline and discharge as the situation requires, but not for the sole reason that the employee is involved in union activities—although employees are expected to work at their assignments during working hours.

Solicitation and Distribution

Many supervisors find themselves perplexed and anxious to take immediate action when employees in their organization come to work wearing buttons and badges that urge employees to vote for a specific union. Similarly, they are also confused when it comes to union leaders soliciting members at the institution premises.

The issue of solicitation is a complex one. Solicitation includes the attempt by union organizers to sign up employees and distribute union campaign material. In general, an employer cannot prevent union organizational activities outside working hours even though the activities take place on the employer's property.

It is also recognized that lunch hours and rest periods are not "working time" despite the fact they may be short or irregularly scheduled and even though employees may be paid for the periods. Generally, an employer can impose a no solicitation rule during working hours so long as the rule is reasonable, necessary for productive operations and not discriminatory. If the rule is valid on its face but is applied in a discriminatory way, or is used as a lever to prevent the workers from exercising their lawful right to organize, the labour laws will call for its elimination.

The Election Process

Finally, once it is determined that there is a *show of interest* the local Labour Relations Board will set an election date and determine the time and place for the election. Usually, the election will be held on institution premises. The voting place is usually determined by mutual agreement between the employer and the union. Present at the polling area is the Board representative who is directly responsible for conducting the election. In addition, the union provides an *observer* and the institution provides an *observer*. The institution's observer may not be a supervisor.

Within a few days after the election has been approved, the board is provided a list of all eligible employees. This list contains the names and addresses of all unit employees. Generally, employees are eligible to vote if they are on the employer's pay-roll for the period immediately prior to the date on which the election is held. In addition, employees who are engaged in an economic strike and have been permanently replaced are still eligible to vote if the election is held within twelve months of the strike. Employees who are on layoff status but have a

"reasonable expectation of re-employment" in the near future have been deemed eligible to vote. Those who have been discharged for cause or who have quit between the date the election was set and the actual voting day are ineligible unless such employees have been discriminatorily discharged.

Employees have the opportunity to vote in secret. They mark a simple ballot *yes* or *no* on the question of whether they wish to be represented by the specific union petitioning. A union must receive a majority of the valid ballots cast in order to be certified. If 50 per cent plus one employee of the employees who voted in the election cast their ballots in favour of the union, the union will become the certified representative of the bargaining unit for the purposes of collective bargaining.

SUMMARY

The following are the key points in a union organizing drive:

1. More employees vote for or against their immediate supervisor than for or against top management, the board of trustees or directors.
2. Unions rarely organize employees; rather, it is administration's poor record in employee relations that drives employees into unions.
3. Institutions that provide all the benefits and conditions of the union shop will not, in most cases, become unionized.
4. There is a marked relationship between worker morale and the extent to which employees feel their boss is interested in discussing work problems with their work group. If the boss is not interested, workers will discuss those problems with outside groups—*in some cases, unions.*
5. Employees who feel group loyalty and pride do not look outside to unions for need fulfillment.
6. Improved managerial practices and the supervisor's attention to the best utilization of people and technology can increase job satisfaction and productivity. Satisfied and fulfilled employees do not look to unions.
7. Unions are looking for *bona fide* issues to use in the organizing drive. Although they will latch on to pretty gripes and perceived injustices, they often look for supervisors who are vulnerable. Such supervisors are usually not employee-centered, have not build up group loyalty, and are not interested in employee needs.

8. Labour unions capitalize on management mistakes.
9. You should not threaten employees or promise them any reward for staying out of the union. Do not interrogate them about their preferences during a union organizing drive. These are unfair labour practices.
10. You can tell employees how the institution feels about unionization. You can share with them the employee disadvantages of belonging to a union.
11. You cannot call employees away from their work areas into your office in order to urge them to vote against the union.

9

Safety-Related Dimensions of Administration

Safety is serious business. The health and welfare of students must be the top priority of vocational educators. We have an obligation to do the best possible job in preparing our students to work safely. Doing so will pay off not only in our own shops and laboratories but also in the workplace—students who learn to work safely in school will be safe workers in business and industry as well.

Safety is also everybody's business. Both instructors and administrators have key roles to play in protecting students and emphasizing the importance that must be placed on safety. Obviously, instructors are on the front line and have the major responsibility for providing a safe and healthful environment for students in vocational education programmes. But administrators are the pace-setters when it comes to the safety and health of students.

SET OF SAFETY POLICIES

Because safety and health are of utmost importance in achieving the goals and objectives of vocational schools, administrators *must* be committed to achieving health and safety standards in all aspects of vocational education programmes. A strong safety philosophy and policy are necessary to support this commitment.

The safety philosophy should commit the school to providing a safe environment and make it clear that instructors are responsible for the well-being of their students. It should also recognize the vital importance of educating all students to work safely. And it should express the belief that all accidents and injuries are preventable.

Out of that philosophy comes a clear set of policies which ought to include several key items :

1. *The facilities and equipment should provide a safe environment in which to work*—If vocational education shops and laboratories are to have a good safety, health, and accident prevention programme, they must begin with safe tools, equipment, procedures and environment.
2. *Working safety should be a condition of employment for all instructors*—The instructors should be expected to accept their responsibility for safety when they join the school staff. Instructors must emphasize the safety of themselves and their students, as well as the safety of the facilities they work in. Rules and procedures must be enforced in order to protect the lives and health of the students.
3. *Adequate safety education should be provided to all students enrolled in vocational education programmes*—It is the responsibility of the instructor to provide this training, and of the administrator to ensure its provision during the very first week of the school term.
4. *Responsibility for preventing personal injuries should rest with all levels of administrators as well as instructors*—Since administrators and instructors share responsibility for all of the activities in the vocational school, both must accept their share of the responsibility for the safety of the students.

There are numerous steps that can be taken to ensure that the goals of the safety and health policies can be met. For one thing, administrators should emphasize the importance of good housekeeping practices and procedures. Keeping shops clean and orderly avoids accidents and helps prevent fires. Make sure that instructors and other staff know what their housekeeping responsibilities are. Plan and conduct housekeeping inspections as you would a safety audit. Remember, the emphasis placed on housekeeping will go a long way in developing a good attitude toward safety.

Administrators must also ensure that instructors are well educated in safety practices and procedures. Use seminars and workshops to assist them in developing a good and comprehensive safety programme.

Invite different agencies into your vocational education facilities to conduct safety audits. Safety auditors might include inspectors from the Occupational Safety and Health Administration, the local fire station chief, insurance company experts and others. Conduct your own walk-through safety audits on a weekly basis as well.

A good maintenance staff is a critical component of a safety programme. Direct them to keep things in good repair at all times. Finally, signs and posters are informative and help to emphasize the importance of a safe and healthful work environment. Administrators who follow these steps will show their commitment to making safety an important part of the school's agenda.

HANDLING HAZARDOUS MATERIALS

The definition of safety has changed dramatically in the last twenty years. The old school believed that safety was a condition of being free from harm and that the only "accident" was a suddenly occurring event which caused immediate injury. The task of safety experts was to keep the work place free from risk by preventing accidents.

More recently, however, the quality of life has become an important safety concern. New workers need to be protected not only from a suddenly occurring event, but also from environmental harm that cannot be seen. This harm, which is potentially greater than that from traditional industrial accidents, often goes un-noticed at the time of exposure, but it may be constantly accumulating, slow moving and invisible. Exposure to such unseen hazards makes itself felt only after a number of years—often to the surprise of the victim.

Business and industrial personnel are not the only persons who need to be concerned about hazardous materials. Toxic chemicals and other dangers are common place in school. Chemistry labs contain all sorts of obvious hazards, art rooms have paints and reducers, and shops produce dust and smoke. Vocational students are handling many of the same substances that manufacturing employees handle. Students deserve the same protection that manufacturing workers have—and they need to know about the hazards they will face when they enter the work force.

Most vocational educators are not completely aware of the dangers associated with the materials they use in their occupations, however, soaps, dyes, tints, cleaning fluids, toxic fumes, and developers, all pose a threat to our health and our environment. Flushing them down the drain does not solve the problem. Many hazardous materials do not break down in nature. When dumped carelessly, they linger in the environment and pose a health hazard to unsuspecting individuals.

In view of the above it becomes mandatory for the administrator to arrange proper hazard communication courses for all instructors within his school. After completing such courses the instructors would be able to:

1. Identify operations in specific work areas where hazardous substances are kept;
2. Demonstrate techniques to detect the presence of hazardous substances;
3. Identify effective techniques for protecting against specific hazards; and
4. Review lesson plans and deliver hazard communication training to secondary and adult vocational education students.

During the course, the teachers would be made to do some research into the nature of hazardous substances existing in their shops or labs. Following this they would determine the proper use, storage, and disposal procedures for each. Finally, they would identify the chemical name of each substance, the hazards it posed, the threshold limit value (exposure limits according to international standards), and personal protection and emergency procedures.

ELEMENTS OF A GOOD SAFETY PROGRAMME

While most vocational administrators are acutely aware of the importance of safety, they more commonly ask questions about what should be included in a safety programme. The following sixteen components make up a comprehensive safety programme:

1. *Require a student acknowledgment form*—At the beginning of the programme, each student signs this form indicating that he or she will follow all safety rules, will only operate tools and equipment after receiving instruction, and will pass all safety tests with a score of 100 per cent.
2. *Require a consent-to-use form*—By signing this form, parents permit their children to operate tools and equipment being used in the programme. This form is often combined with the student acknowledgment so that parents are aware of what is expected of students from the outset.
3. *Administer safety tests*—Written tests should cover general safety rules and specific safety practices. Students must also demonstrate their ability to use hazardous tools, materials, and equipment by successfully completing performance tests. They must score 100 per cent on all safety tests. Once completed, these tests are placed in each student's file.

4. *Post general safety rules*—General safety rules are those which apply at all times throughout the classroom and laboratory. Examples include stipulations for wearing safety glasses, a policy on horseplay, procedures for entering and leaving the laboratory, guidelines for appropriate dress and housekeeping requirements.
5. *Post specific safety procedures*—Specific safety procedures are those which apply to a specific tool, piece of equipment or process. For example, a carpentry classroom should have safety rules for operating the table saw posted on or near the saw.
6. *Enforce safety rules*—While it is critical to establish general and specific safety rules, enforcing these rules is even more important. It is well known that many vital rules and regulations, initiated with very sincere and good intentions fail to deliver if not enforced strictly.
7. *Conduct safety inspections*—In the presence of your students and staff, you should conduct periodic safety inspections. Develop an inspection checklist or use one of the many available from various safety and health organizations. These checklists include the condition of the laboratory, emergency exists, equipment, walking surfaces, storage areas, ventilation, lighting, fire alarms and extinguisher and many other items.
8. *Establish emergency procedures*—In conjunction with the state educational authorities, you must establish procedures to follow in the event of a serious accident. Should these authorities be informed in the event of a serious laboratory or workshop floor accident? Is a health professional available at all working hours? Do you have the authority to call an ambulance? What should the students and instructors do in the event of an accident? As an administrator you must ensure that you have a clear-cut and unambiguous emergency plan in place.
9. *Maintain a first aid kit*—While administrators are usually prohibited from distributing medicine, you can maintain a first aid kit in the event of a serious accident. The kit should contain items such as bandages, antiseptic ointment, gauze and tape. Talk with a health professional for more information.
10. *Document safety instruction*—While administrators are unable to prevent all accidents and injuries, they are expected to establish a concrete safety programme which will help prevent accidents and, in the event of legal action, serve as proof that

the administrator made every reasonable attempt to provide a safe environment. Hence, safety must figure prominently in your school's instructional programme through information sheets, notes, lesson plans, audio-visual presentations, demonstrations based on job or procedure sheets, guest speakers and tests.

11. *Keep equipment in good operating condition*—Safe operating condition means that all guards are in place, equipment operates to manufacturer's specifications, periodic inspections are conducted, and preventive maintenance schedules are followed. You should be able to provide records of all equipment inspections, maintenance and repair.
12. *Ensure that all laboratories and workshops are safe*—Safety inspection can help you identify areas that need improvement.
13. *Ensure that all accidents are reported and investigated*—Your students and instructors must report *all* accidents. You must then investigate each accident to determine the cause and identify procedures for preventing similar accidents in the future. All accident reports should be filed for future reference.
14. *Implement effective safety supervision*—The majority of accidents result from human error and many of these occur in laboratories because of inappropriate student behaviour and inadequate instructor supervision. Ensure that teachers remain in the classroom and laboratory area to supervise students. Only in emergency situations should students be left in a laboratory without teacher supervision.
15. *Instruct teaching staff to model safe behaviour*—Ask your teachers to demonstrate an attitude that makes safety a priority, *i.e.* by wearing personal protective equipment, using tools and materials safely, and following all safety rules.
16. *Secure liability insurance*—While legal action against teachers or administrators is rare, it does happen. Liability insurance policies are relatively inexpensive and are available through professional associations such as state or national vocational association. Coverage may also be available through your school board or through a personal liability provider.

When all sixteen of these points are in place, fewer accidents will occur, injuries will be less severe, and students will be able to work and study in a safe environment. In the event of a legal question as well, the

administrator will be able to demonstrate that every effort was made to provide for the safety of the vocational student.

SUMMARY

For the vocational administrator, safety must be the number one priority. Not even the quality of student work and learning activities is more important. Work habits which prevent accidents and guard against personal injuries *must be taught*. Administrators cannot afford to assume that students will automatically know what safety procedures to follow.

The layout of the shop or laboratory must be well planned and safety must be a built-in feature. Adequate space is necessary to allow proper placement of equipment and roomy aisles for traffic from one area to another. The location of gas, water, lighting, electrical devices, compressed air, and ventilation system must be carefully thought out.

Students need instruction on safety practices, procedures, and regulations beginning on the first day of class. Orientation should cover general safety policies, procedures, and precautions when operating specific machines and equipment, and the importance of good housekeeping practices. Written safety materials must be available to the students at all times. Also, a series of written and performance tests be administered to make sure students understand safety procedures and their importance. Students must also learn fire prevention, the classes of fires, types of extinguishers and how to use them, and where they are located in the shop or laboratory.

All accidents are preventable, and vocational administrators have a responsibility to protect their students and staff. This requires continuous supervision, proper guards on all machines and equipment, the wearing of personal protective gear, proper storage and handling of hazardous materials, and regular checks to ensure that all tools and equipment are in good working order at all times.

Finally, administrators must investigate every accident immediately and keep records on all such incidents. Learning from past accident reports is the best way to prevent future mishaps.

10

Administrator's Role in Improving the Skills and Adaptability of the National Workforce

The wealth of a nation rests mostly on the quality of its workforce, not on the quantity of its natural resources. But such a workforce must be prepared, and prepared well, in order to cope with the changing demands of the labour market. Not only will a nation have to build a strong workforce which can keep up with technological developments but which will also be able to plan and show initiative to develop and produce new technologies, new products and new services. Failing this, it shall have to make do with second place standing.

But training of such a workforce requires more than simply developing the memory. Trainers will help develop personal skills, contribute to master professional gestures but they must develop reflective capacities within their students or apprentices. They must also help them to develop good working habits. Overall, they must encourage them to pursue their training and to always try to understand the meaning of their actions. The privileged relationship between a trainer and his trainees is a unique means to pass on these values which help to produce qualified workers.

Today, any one country is only a part of the global village which the world has become, and vocational educators must, at the very least, keep abreast of a global economy in which technology leads the way and sets the pace. Increasingly, and in every field of economic activity, routine work will be performed by robots, leaving the interesting jobs to people able to perform as doers, but also and especially, as thinkers. A forward looking nation will require its manpower not only to be able to follow-up with the fast changing technology but to prepare for those changes, to contribute to their coming. Vocational administrators need to become involved in such matters and to provide leadership in this area. In order to do so, they must have clear comprehension of such issues as the dichotomy between academic and vocational education,

the importance of timely career guidance, and the significance of technical-vocational education in a global economy era.

THE DICHOTOMY BETWEEN ACADEMIC AND VOCATIONAL EDUCATION

The dichotomy between academic and vocational education is proving detrimental to the survival of secondary school vocational programmes. While academic programmes are perceived as "real" education and considered as ladders to future success, secondary vocational programmes are subjected to criticism, as they have:

- been the recipients of the less able students
- used curricula that are not competency based
- directed programmes that lack performance measures
- not evaluated their programmes on a regular basis
- been separated from general education

Many policy-makers in education also do not believe that vocational education is as equally useful for preparing a student for life as is so-called general education. They persist with the false dichotomy despite the results of recent research which has conclusively pointed out that any dichotomy between academic and vocational education is unwarranted and outmoded.

A study by Paul Campbell and Nancy Pules has revealed just how false this dichotomy is.[1] The study looked at what happened to 100 students as they moved through their required years of public schooling and into the workforce or further education across North America. The results of the study showed very similar success in future additional education and obtaining work regardless of whether the students graduated from the general, academic or vocational school.

If we were to eliminate vocational education from secondary schools we would not live up to our responsibilities as educators in:

- providing every citizen with sufficient education so that he/she can enter employment
- encouraging every citizen to undertake education leading to employment before discontinuing full time or formal education
- providing an environment that encourages learning
- removing artificial and unnecessary barriers to an education

that enhances employment
- ensuring smooth transition from school to work
- helping people become life-long learners.

To fulfill these responsibilities we need the kind of vocational education that is relevant to the needs of people with a wide range of abilities and enable them to bridge the gap between so-called "academic" and so-called "vocational" studies. We need to realize that *all* subjects are potentially *general* in nature. It is the purpose or objective of the person enrolled that makes them vocational. An English course is likely to be vocational for a writer as it is for a stenographer.

Vocational administrators must understand that the kind of vocational education for the future will not have a narrow "training" focus, but will aim to do a number of things so that students in the programmes will:

1. have acquired specific skills to enter an occupation.
2. have a general occupational intelligence concerning the roles of other people.
3. be intelligent consumers of goods and have a knowledge of materials, products, tools, workmanship, and design.
4. understand the national and international economic systems.
5. obtain information on many careers, sample some careers, and be able to choose one which will be interesting and rewarding to them personally.
6. have obtained a rounded general education, including both academic and vocational skills.
7. know how to advance in a given occupation and have the right attitude to advance by doing further studies.
8. be equipped with a means of getting a temporary job while pursuing other life or career goals.
9. have the ability to work with others and function as part of an organization.
10. develop an avocational interest, such as a hobby.
11. have acquired sufficient theory in their trade/business area to allow them to continue to advance by taking special courses.
12. be able to solve problems related to their area of business/industry (*i.e.* be creative).
13. have developed a real feeling of achievement by producing tangible evidence of their studies.
14. understand how technical objects work and the effects of technology on today's world.

One note of caution. In his bid to change, let the administrator not forget the idea that the learner must be active in the learning process, not passive. Personal experience and practice in a variety of contexts should be related to more abstract concepts. First hand experience coupled with abstract concepts optimizes learning. Vocational education should be used to make general education concrete and understandable. Furthermore, vocational programmes should be developmental, not terminal.

THE IMPORTANCE OF TECHNICAL-VOCATIONAL EDUCATION IN A GLOBAL ECONOMY ERA

The industrial revolution in early industrialized nations made it clear, that technical-vocational education was essential to provide the skilled workforce which would produce the goods and services in their society. Whether one examines the British, German, French, or American vocational education delivery system, it becomes apparent that in each case, the apprenticeship system was augmented by both public and private schools for providing vocational education graduates to create the skilled workforce. These countries benefited very quickly by producing goods and services not only for domestic purposes but for international markets as well. There are strong national commitments in many industrialized countries today in apprenticeship training. Young workers have the opportunity to work and receive specialized training. This is a very old delivery of vocational training yet it is to a nation's interest and certainly to an industry's long term benefit, to enable the young worker not only to be more productive but also provide the early training that allows a young worker to progress to more responsible and complex tasks.

Still other industrialized nations are recognizing the value of continuous upgrading of skills as more complex processes, equipment, and materials are being added. In Taiwan, for example, the training centres operating under the Ministry of Labour provide training and retraining of industrial workers to maintain a competitive workforce for their industries.

In the United States, young persons have an opportunity to participate in job employment and training programmes which are also sponsored by the Department of Labour and then join apprenticeship programmes after completing short intensive technical training.

Both Canada and Germany have retained strong apprenticeship training closely integrated with their public training institutes.

What is becoming apparent in most industrialized nations, is that technical training of the workforce will require a national commitment

as the goods and services which are in demand require a greater skill and expectation of quality by the consumer. For many decades, the industrialized nations in the free world had enormous market opportunities because of the dependence on the industrialized nations for many manufactured goods and services.

It was in the national interest for governments to creat legislation favourable to ensuring a ready supply of skilled and semi-skilled workers for the industrial sector. Industrialists also were critically aware of the importance of well prepared technical workforce as investments in sophisticated equipment and processes were introduced in the manufacturing and service sectors. This was particularly apparent during the World War II period when production of goods and services for defence was also critical.

Rapid Industrialization in NIC

The NIC or newly industrialized countries had to make a rapid transition from a labour intensive agricultural economy to a semi-skilled and skilled workforce for an industrial, export-oriented economy. Faced with a world economy, the NICs had also had to advance very rapidly and adapt to the use of high technology whether this involved robots, computers, programmable controllers, laser optics, ultrasonic waves, or whatever is being effectively and competitively used in the highly developed industrialized nations.

The new industrial countries have developed their industrial sector since World War II and have invested extensively in both vocational education and vocational retraining. For example, Taiwan has invested more than 13 per cent of its GNP in education, and technical-vocational education is pursued by 70 per cent of its high school students. Also, extensive provisions are made for continued technical-vocational studies at the Institutes of Technology up through the graduate levels. Japan has a similar emphasis. The highly industrialized nations are challenged as they have never been challenged before for their share of world economy markets by the NICs.

The Plight of the Underdeveloped Nations

Underdeveloped nations find it extremely difficult to create the necessary infrastructure without a competent workforce to attract industrial development. Even, with our knowledge of technology transfer, unless

we have reliable communication and transportation networks, consistent water and electrical supplies (and other parts of the infrastructural network including banking, commerce and marketing), few investors will show interest. Moreover, it takes skilled people to install, maintain and provide such services before any industrial developer will risk capital investment.

In underdeveloped countries, frequently there is a lack of quality vocational education and vocational retraining beyond that generally needed by government services. Furthermore, there is also a critical shortage of middle management personnel who understand the indigenous population values, norms and work habits. To compound the problem, there is also the fear of automation which, by making the mostly unskilled labour redundant, may deprive them of their livelihood.

Automation

The influence of automation has not diminished the need for semi-skilled and skilled workers. Rather it has increased the demand for such workers as the more routine and simple tasks are automated. The investments in automation coupled with better prepared and educated skilled workforce has led to greater productivity and higher GNP. The threat of automation has been with us for some time, yet it is not as fearsome anymore. For example, the reaper machine displaced many reapers in the agriculture sector. Yet, the modern-day combine not only reaps the crop, but threshes it, stores the grain, and transports it until it is transferred to a truck which conveys it to the market or central storage.

Automation is also viewed as a positive feature of today's industry. It has provided the means to remove the drudgery of working in hostile environments, doing repetitive, monotonous jobs. More importantly, it has cut costs of our goods and services. The automated and computerized banking, the robot welders and paint sprayers, and computer voice mail, each are altering the workplace.

Today's flexible manufacturing allows for small batch production, lesser consumption of materials, reduced inventories, reduced warehousing, and less time between production and sales. Such equipment is more capital intensive and thereby, while it reduces the need for production workers, it does require more technically competent individuals to maintain such equipment operational and to prevent down time. Obviously, if industry equips a worker with an improved machine, the output will be greater. However, for the unskilled, automation reduces one's prospects of continuous employment.

In the last analysis, automation has led to increased emphasis on extended vocational education preparation so that automated equipment could be built, operated and maintained. With industrial type computers being rapidly expanded, we should anticipate that automation will continue to reduce the opportunities in industry for the unskilled, but increase employment opportunities for the skilled.

Multinational Company Development

In recent years many large companies have found sufficient markets abroad to build plants in such countries. Others were attracted by lower labour costs, less burdensome taxes, lower energy costs, and other reasons. The experience by such companies has been generally, mixed. In some industrially developed countries, technical-vocational education was well developed and the indigenous workforce was available to provide the pool of skills and services necessary. On the other hand, in lesser industrially developed countries, the experience was not so encouraging. The problem ultimately lay in finding appropriately skilled people to run the operation, and invariably it was linked to a low status accorded to technical-vocational education by educators and politicians in these countries.

World Economy

After the industrial revolution in many of the countries, there was a large world market to supply necessary goods and technical services. Britain, France, Germany, Canada, United States, and other nations experienced growing economies and increased opportunities to market manufactured goods and to provide marketing and technical services. After World War II, continued prosperity still kept the industrial generators running and multinational companies increased dramatically through the next three decades.

Soon the competition for markets diminished as newly industrialized nations (NIC) began to compete for a share of the world market. Economic summit meetings seldom yielded insights in how to deal with a world economy. Huge deficits, changing monetary values, high interest rates, changing consumer patterns, complex supply and demand economic relationships, high costs of energy, rising costs of national defence, rapid population growth, and growing national inter-dependence, all impact, not only our national economics, but mandate the recognition that we are

faced with a situation in which no one common market can control or manipulate at will the world economy.

There is a need to first recognize that a world economy may rely more on cooperation rather than competition. The Ford Escort, for example, is manufactured in Great Britain and Germany. However, fifteen countries provide the manufactured component parts. This car is sold in the world market and represents the largest sales model for Ford Motor Company.

The elevation of the living standards throughout the world will produce a demand for more consumer goods and services. There is a second vision that must not elude us. That is, the world economy must rest on the foundation of world development, and investment in education is a key element of such developmental process. Its importance is reflected in the growing recognition, since the early 1960s, that investing in both formal and informal education and training provides and enhances the skills, knowledge, attitudes, and motivation necessary for economic and social development.

Development of human resource, and most specifically, technical-vocational education, is as critical as the development of other sectors if we are to ultimately create a world economy that can sustain a tolerable standard of living for the masses.

Labour Market Information

Without access to reliable and up-to-date information on available training programmes and employment opportunities, many vocationally trained people will be unaware of courses to upgrade their skills. Jobs for which unemployed graduates will be qualified may also continue to go unfilled. There is, therefore, the need for improved *dissemination* of labour market information—starting in the school system. There is also the need for the governments to make employees, employers, students, educators, and others aware of training and skills development programmes through public information campaigns. A more comprehensive and up-to-date catalogue of training programmes, possibly on line, will also be one effective means to increase public participation in labour market programmes.

The *quality* of labour market data must also be improved. Timely and reliable labour market data is essential to understanding emerging skill and occupational requirements and to the design of quality training programmes that effectively meet these requirements. It is also vital to

our ability to measure both current levels of industry training and industry's progress in meeting its training objectives over time. The need for reliable local labour market data will also be critical to the success of labour market programmes, designed and delivered at the community level.

There is also the need for *monitoring* of various labour market programmes. Effective programme evaluation techniques are essential to measure and monitor the success of individual labour market programmes, particularly since the objectives these programmes are designed to meet often change in response to shifting social or economic conditions. Improved measures to ensure, on an ongoing basis, that current programmes are continuing to meet their objectives are, therefore, imperative.

CAREER GUIDANCE AND COUNSELLING

For the past two decades, policy-planners everywhere have been rediscovering vocational education as the major instrument available to develop productive citizens and a productive work force. It is also argued that enhanced productivity is not possible without educational excellence. Yet it seems to be an over simplification of the complexity of the educational process in general, suggesting that just a few key ingredients will give us both the personal and academic excellence sought.

What is frequently suggested is the modification of the structure and organization of schooling, without addressing the diversity of student characteristics and needs. Yet, to achieve educational excellence, schools must embrace the many learning styles and motivations of students, even those who have been on the margin of society. And in a vocational system, more than anywhere else, it is the guidance and counselling staff that can aid in meeting this challenge.

Of course all school staff help meet student needs, but guidance and counselling staff are uniquely equipped to develop student commitment to personal excellence. This is accomplished by helping students learn about themselves, their intelligence, and their strengths and purposes. Accurate self-knowledge is pivotal to students' use of educational opportunities, since it gives them the confidence that applying their skills and talents constructively will lead to meaningful and desired outcomes. But our educational system does not emphasize guidance and counselling for all students, which is why progress toward excellence is not as rapid as we all wish. To solve this problem, vocational administrators

must ensure that formal guidance exposure is provided to all students in order to reduce the drop-out rate and to equip the students with needed coping skills for today's world, and transitional skills for making a smooth move from school to the workplace.

Reducing Drop-out Rate

Today, approximately a quarter of all students entering a vocational programme drop-out within the first few months of the academic session. Even worse, many of these youths not only drop-out of school, they also drop-out of life. Close to 50 per cent of these drop-outs will disconnect from society entirely, turning instead to drugs, crime, suicide and other outlets. Clearly, this situation demand immediate attention from the guidance and counselling staff who, with the aid of proper strategies, can help in salvaging many lives.

For those students who seem drop-out prone, many different strategies are available to encourage retention. The common feature of these strategies can be summed up by the five "I's":

1. Identify potential drop-outs while they are still in the primary stage of the programme.
2. Inform students of the different vocational programmes available at the same school.
3. Individualize the educational approach for potential drop-outs, focussing not only on academic achievements, but also on personal and work-related needs.
4. Implement courses in job search skills. These courses should teach students how to provide potential employers with information about themselves.
5. Involve a variety of persons in a drop-out prevention team—teachers, counsellors, parents and community agencies.

Providing Coping Skills for Today's World

It is unfortunate that although most vocational schools provide adequate vocational skills, they fail to emphasize certain basic skills so crucial in today's complex living. These skills have to do with the individual ability to:

1. achieve at work
2. cope with non-work

3. reach out for, and attain further education
4. deal with personal affairs and problems
5. cope with, and take advantage of leisure time
6. participate in community affairs
7. put family affairs in context with other life goals

How can these goals of self-awareness and self-fulfillment be met? Schools can help students acquire a base of personal information that provides purpose and direction to their schooling. In large measure, the vehicle for providing such personal information is a comprehensive career assessment programme. Aptitude assessment and interest measurement not only help monitor progress, they can also help students make informal choices, set personal standards, and determine performance areas in which they feel successful and comfortable. In this sense, these forms of self-knowledge permit students to approach educational and job opportunities with a feeling of personal commitment and anticipation. It allows them to see these opportunities as avenues leading to personal goals rather than as individual hurdles over which they leap without a clear sense of reward.

Even more important, objective information allows one to base goals on true capabilities rather than on a self-image of "winner" or "loser", which often arises when viewing grades alone. Schools striving for excellence can neutralize subjective messages about being a winner or loser by providing personal information that is objective, comprehensive and competently interpreted.

Guidance providers can emphasize the link between educational excellence and test information. They can explain to students and staff alike that student decision-making is fueled by information. They can clarify the fact that career choices should not be made impulsively, but must be a sequential narrowing and specifying of choice options as various psychological and occupational information is translated into a self-concept system and matching educational and occupational opportunities.

Schools, therefore, can encourage students to pursue personal excellence in whatever area of strength or talent they possess. Administrators can encourage their school to provide this information as early as possible, so that students can choose options that broaden their horizons, not close them—options that reinforce the opportunity for rewards, not avoid them.

Providing Transitional Skills

One of the most difficult transitions that takes place in life is when a young person moves from school to the workplace. The transition process can be improved considerably when the school provides special help and information to students that aids them in navigating the job market.

Youth are frequently not aware of employer's standards for hiring and job performance. Counsellors can let students know that the following interview and application factors have the greatest negative influence on employers' decisions to hire:

1. below average reading ability
2. falsification of the application
3. frequent job changes, quits or layoffs
4. high absenteeism on last job
5. low effort on last job
6. no prior work experience

Students also need to know that the following interview and application factors have the greatest positive influence on employers' decisions to hire:

1. clean and neat appearance at the interview
2. interest shown during the interview by asking questions about the job
3. interest shown after the interview by calling the employer
4. neat and correctly completed application
5. bio-data attached to the job application

Experience shows that students also benefit from the following assistance:

1. Inform students (particularly drop-out prone youth) that completion of a diploma, certificate, or degree will positively affect their employment chances and their earning potential.
2. Encourage students to (a) obtain some work experience while in vocational school, and (b) search for employment after graduation in an occupational area related to their vocational training.
3. Encourage students who are drop-out prone, bored, or frustrated to seek career guidance. Make them feel welcome to drop-in to

> the counsellor's office whenever they feel dejected and see their future as hopeless.

Additionally, effective counselling support services are vital to the success of labour market programmes. Counselling is the best way to identify those most likely to benefit from labour market programmes and those most at risk of experiencing long-term unemployment. Early identification, especially through counselling at the time of notice of job loss, will allow individuals about to lose their jobs to be quickly enrolled in retraining programmes—before their skills and morale start to deteriorate.

SUMMARY

This chapter brings together the role of vocational administrator in improving the skills and adaptability of the national workforce through the medium of his/her school, and deals mainly with the serious topic of optimizing investment in human resources and strategies for achieving excellence in vocational education. Administrators must recognize the high purposes of this type of education and make plans of action that can be applicable to individual countries and regions. As the globe shrinks, the investment in education of every individual may be the most critical factor to improved life styles, livelihoods and peace on our globe. The opposite polar position is one of the human suffering, poverty and accumulated armaments.

The chapter begins with the statement that there is a false dichotomy that exists between two areas of secondary schools (academic and vocational), along with the belief that vocational education is not as useful in preparing a student for life as is so-called academic or general education. These notions are totally outmoded. It is absurd to suggest that general knowledge for its own sake is somehow superior to useful knowledge. To ensure smooth transition from school to work we need the kind of vocational education that is relevant to the needs of people with a wide range of abilities and enables them to bridge the gap between the so-called "academic" and "vocational" studies.

It is suggested that administrators must comprehend the critical importance of technical-vocational education in a global economy era. They must also familiarize themselves with the evolution of this type of education in the industrialized nations of the West, and later in the NICs or newly industrialized countries of the East. They must also take note of

the influence of automation on the employment opportunities for the skilled and unskilled workers.

Lastly, vocational administrators must recognize that the achievement of educational excellence is a function of student commitment to personal excellence. When we have the commitment, we have individual action directed to effective decision-making, planning and preparation. This demands career guidance, occupational counselling, and assessment.

Educational excellence, then, is shaped by and is reciprocal to the confidence of students in their ability to pursue programmes that challenge their abilities, provide access to opportunity, and rest upon self-knowledge and informed choice. Without student commitment, we can have reforms and change that bring us no closer than before to educational excellence. To achieve excellence, we must remember the key ingredient—the students, and their commitment to their future.

Reference

1. Campbell, Paul and Nancy Pulçs. What Happens to High School Students? *Vocational Education Journal*, October 1986, pp. 21-22.

11

Administrator's Role in Vocational Education of the Future

If we were to examine the future of any aspect of education, such as education for vocational life, we can do only by projecting and interpolating facts which already exist. It also seems logical, in considering such a topic, to look for evidence that will throw light upon questions such as the following: (1) In the future, will the majority of our youth continue their education beyond the higher secondary school and thus be able, in most cases, to defer preparation for work to this later period? (2) What will the occupation of the future be like? (3) Will they require much preparation? (4) Will the nature and extent of the preparation required to pursue the occupations permit such preparation to be postponed beyond the secondary school?

If answers to such questions lead us, as administrators, to conclude that vocational education has a place in planning for the high school of the future, then we must ask: (1) How great will be the need for vocational education? (2) What characteristics will such education have? (3) How can it best be organized and conducted?

We are all aware that the holding power of our secondary school has been increasing, that more young people are staying in school longer. Most of us are also aware that a greater and greater portion of our young people are going on into higher education. We are told to expect an explosive growth in college enrolments in the years ahead.

Not a few educational planners have accepted as a fact the conclusion that in the future all vocational education can be, and will be, deferred beyond the high school because all, or nearly all young people requiring such education will be found in some programmes of higher education. This conclusion assumes, of course, that the decision can be made in terms of when the student is available to be prepared and that no other factors will affect the decision.

FACTS CONCERNING NEEDS FOR VOCATIONAL EDUCATION IN HIGHER SECONDARY SCHOOLS

In spite of the improvement in the holding power of our higher secondary schools, a large number of youth belonging to the 17-19 year age group in our population are not enrolled in any school programmes. We know that nearly all the young men not in school, and a large per cent of the young women, were in the labour market; except for the armed services, there was no place else for most of them to be. These per cents will surely decrease in the years ahead. Yet there is no solid evidence to indicate that the *majority* of our youth will, in the foreseeable future, continue their education for a substantial period beyond the higher secondary level. Even allowing for increase in the rate of growth of post-secondary education far beyond that of any known index, the majority of our youth will not, for many years to come, receive any education for work if it is deferred beyond the higher secondary school.

At least two other factors will play a part in limiting the formal education of the majority of young people to that secured in the high school. One is the serious and unrelieved labour shortage which will be a most important economic and social feature of the next two decades. This shortage is readily predictable from the age distribution of our present population. As a result great pressure will be exerted on every individual capable of contributing to the output of goods and services to induce him to make such a contribution. Despite all that can be done through counselling and advice, large numbers of young people will find, at the completion of their high-school education that the opportunities for earning are too attractive to be resisted. We may hope that they will be motivated, and will have the opportunity, to continue their education on a part-time basis.

Another factor bearing upon the proper placement of vocational education is the rapid increase in the amount of basic and technical preparation required for success in the jobs of the future. This requirement can very well increase the necessity for basic occupational preparation at the higher secondary level. Assuming that we can persuade fairly large numbers of young people to continue their education for at least two years beyond the higher secondary school, it becomes increasingly doubtful that this span of time will be sufficient to complete the preparation needed for the jobs of the future. On the contrary, it seems more and more likely that, to provide anything like the preparation needed, the basic elements of the preparation will have to begin not

later than the eleventh year of school.

Wherever serious studies have been made by economists, industrialists, sociologists, government agencies, or educators, the facts all point to this conclusion: while there will be a continuing expansion of vocational education at the post-secondary level, to suppose that the need for vocational education offerings in the higher secondary school will diminish is to make a serious mistake. Rather than eliminating our concern for the vocational preparation of youth at this level, our higher secondary school will be forced to concern itself, more and more, with meeting this need, at least in the upper years.

THE NATURE OF WORLD OF WORK IN THE FUTURE

If the high school of the future must play a part in the direct preparation of youth for careers, it is essential that those who plan educational programmes understand, much more clearly than many of them do now, what the world of work is like today, what has already happened to change it, and what it will be like in the foreseeable future. The word "automation" has become widely used and we have already discussed it in the preceding chapter. It is associated in the public mind with new and magical methods for producing goods. It is that and much more. Few people, even those engaged in programmes of automation, fully understand the implication of this phenomenon, which have been revealed by some of our most brilliant economists and sociologists. No educational administrator of the future can afford to be ignorant of the full meaning of the effects which are already flowing from the truly revolutionary set of concepts described by the term "automation".

So far as preparation for careers is concerned, what it means is a massive upgrading of the skills required by the entire labour force of the country. The unskilled worker of yesterday has already disappeared from the industrial scene, never to return. Already the processes have begun which will upgrade the semi-skilled and the skilled machine-operators of today into the highly skilled and knowledgeable technicians of tomorrow. And the term "skill" must be redefined because the skills of one era are dead and the skills of the new era are just emerging. A visitor to the industrial plants that have begun to adopt these new processes is struck by the small number of workers actually on the production floor, and these workers will become fewer and fewer. In plants such as power-generating stations or oil refineries, practically no workers are in sight, but large numbers of persons are working behind

the scenes in new, highly skilled jobs, as machine builders, machine installers, instrument technicians, trouble shooters, testers, data-processors, designers, draftsmen, programmers and mathematicians. These are the industrial jobs, and the prototypes of other jobs, of the future.

Village agriculture has long been a declining field of employment. Of all the young men born in the villages today, one of every two must find employment in non-agriculture sector. Soon two of every three will find it necessary to leave the village farm to earn a living. The application of scientific principles to crop production and livestock breeding, plus mechanization of farm processes, has brought about a complete revolution in agriculture, even in the third-world nations. These changes in agriculture result in constantly shrinking opportunities for careers, and the careers are steadily becoming more technical and managerial in nature. The entire programmes of vocational agriculture in our schools will have to be re-examined in light of these facts.

The concepts associated with automation will probably have a greater impact upon office and business occupations than upon production processes. This fact appears to be little understood by leaders in commercial and business education. The only job below the managerial which will ultimately survive in the business office may be that of the private secretary. This fact must be reckoned with any consideration of vocational preparation for girls in the future.

Many types of jobs which have required few workers in the past will use significantly large numbers in the future. Some of these are outgrowths of a better standard of living, the widespread distribution of leisure, and our changing patterns of life. An illustration is the amazing increase in activity in the tourism trade, which has created thousands of new jobs in the area of catering and hotel management. This illustration could be multiplied many times.

There will, of course, be opportunities for great numbers of people in types of jobs which do not exist at all today. Whatever the mind of man visualizes today, the genius of modern science can turn into functioning facts tomorrow. The important fact for vocational educators is that, as these new type of jobs come into existence, they will demand a level of preparation which is considerably more thorough and more technical than has ever been required in the past.

These few brief glimpses into the future of the world of work will suffice to indicate that the working world will be far different from that in which many of us have laboured. Many of the details are, of course,

unknown at this time, but the main trends are unmistakable. The vocational administrator can easily base his plans for vocational education for the future upon these clear trends.

MEANING OF THESE TRENDS FOR VOCATIONAL EDUCATION

These trends show that careers of the future, at all levels, will require people with more, better and different education. They will require trained brain power to an extent never imagined during the earlier period of our industrial and social development, and surely not fully appreciated today. The preparation for these careers cannot consist in developing skills in "gadgeteering". Even in routine jobs, automation will require ability to think, a trained imagination, and good judgment, plus some skill in logical methods, some mathematical understanding, and some ability well above the elementary level to read and write.

Viewed superficially, these facts may lead to the belief that a so-called good general education will be the only preparation needed for such a future. Penetrating analysis shows, however, that this is not the case. The quality of our general education, as well as that of other aspects of the educational programme, will, of course, need to be considerably enhanced. In addition, the higher secondary school of the future will have to provide, for the majority of its students, direct and applied education for the new vocations. Recent research has shown that among most young people, especially those of superior capacity, the career objective becomes an effective central strand in educational motivation. The education of these young people does not proceed best in isolated disregard of lifetime occupational activities.

In terms of the future, then, we may conclude that vocational education in our schools will become almost wholly technical education. The typical worker of the future, excluding those who can be unquestionably classified as professional, will be the technician, male or female (and the connotation of the world "technician" will be broadened). Technioians in the past have been thought of as akin to engineers, although on a lower level. In the future they will be found in many areas of occupational life in addition to engineering and industry. The technician is a person who works at a job which requires technical knowledge and technical skill but little manual skill. The technician's work assignments are usually made by professionals, under whose supervision the technician works. Supervision, however, is loose rather than close, and an important characteristic of the successful technician

is the ability to work independently under broad assignments.

The technical education which is being described here will need to be offered in terms of broad areas of preparation, which provide directly for occupational life but go much beyond the requirements of the first job. It will not be enough to prepare solely for the first job, because the first job, and most succeeding jobs which the worker of tomorrow will hold, will change radically, and often. Illustrations of such areas of technical preparation might be the areas of chemistry, of mechanical technology, of electrical technology, of health services, of business controls and analysis, of food preparation and service, and many others.

Over the years, vocational education has met its responsibilities successfully in countries wherever it has been permitted to develop properly. Where it has not been used as a dumping ground for those who did not fit well in other programmes, it has generally served well the youth it has enrolled. At a few times and in a few places it has, in its attempts to be practical, become too narrow and shortsighted. Vocational education has always been more concerned with the total development and welfare of the pupil than its detractors have been aware of or willing to admit. Nevertheless, formulas of the past will not suffice for tomorrow. Those with the interests of technical-vocational education at heart must be willing to review its place in the total programme of education. There must be a willingness to reconsider, and if necessary to modify, the legislation upon which it has so long depended for direction as well as for strength, to seek appropriate changes in its pattern of administration and organization, in the nature of its offerings, in the qualifications of teachers and administrators. It must be sufficiently flexible to adapt itself quickly and frequently to the needs of the economy, of the society, and of the individuals who compose the society. Those who lead technical-vocational education at all levels of the school programme must be sensitive to the changes described. They cannot afford to stick doggedly to a programme of training for skills which are disappearing or for occupations which are dying or dead.

HOW SHALL VOCATIONAL EDUCATION OF THE FUTURE BE PROVIDED?

Let's begin by re-emphasizing that our concern with career need not be illiberal or narrow. Concern with career is in accord with the ancient educational tradition and with the highest cultivation of student abilities. Neither its devotees nor its detractors should suppose that there is

anything in the nature of vocational education which requires to be narrow or more limited than is needful in the best interests of the students. The issue of vocational versus liberal, or vocation versus culture has always been a false one, and future events will make discussions of it seem more sterile and unprofitable with each passing year.

Today, most countries of the world are aspiring to ascend heights whose upper limit is not yet measurable, and at an accelerated rate of speed. The key to this rise is technology. For the individual, the key to success in the technological future is his readiness and preparation to take part in it. Administrators of technical-vocational education everywhere must provide for their youth the career preparation for this kind of future. Among the important features of programmes of technical-vocational education in the future, will be the following:

1. Youth enrolled in technical-vocational curriculums will participate simultaneously in the same full programmes of general education available to all youth. This participation is quite possible and is being accomplished in several places.
2. Technical-vocational curriculums will be planned so that they can, at one and the same time, offer terminal education for those who desire to give their entire school day to this programme and offer college-preparatory education for those desirous of, and capable of going further.
3. Courses and curriculums will emerge from the direct requirements of occupational life. Consequently the curriculum planners must be in continuous and understanding contact with the world of work and with research agencies which study occupations.
4. Curriculums will be broad and forward-looking yet thoroughly realistic. They would also be more rigorous, with high standards.
5. Vocational education teachers will be recruited from among experienced practitioners of the technical activities which they will teach.
6. Vocational education teachers will be well prepared to teach mathematics, science, economics, sociology, psychology and communications as these subjects are applied in a variety of work environments. Vocational education classrooms and laboratories will be filled with references and activities students can use to develop interpersonal communication and other people-oriented skills.

7. All vocational teachers will be in a position to guarantee that their graduates are proficient in word and information processing, languages arts, records, financial management, economic fundamentals, market and project research and customer service.
8. Teachers and students will know how to network with international markets, operate multipurpose computer terminals, use voice-recognition computer systems, operate electronic conferencing systems and use software packages to create, manage and disseminate information.
9. Teachers will use team building methodologies—teaching in groups, drawing heavily on community and school resources and the help of expert assistants. They will have time to plan, reflect, evaluate, and refine lessons and approaches related to individual student needs.
10. Teaching methods will include case studies, computer simulations, problem solving, creative-thinking exercises and student group presentations. Lecture-style pedagogy, rote memorization, and textbook-driven course work will be discouraged. Data and logic will be the basis for business and industry case decision making.
11. The community at large will be in true partnership with the education of its youth and adults. Increasing numbers of students will be involved with quality cooperative school-industry training programmes.
12. The vocational student population will be much more culturally diverse and female, and these students will have better access to vocational education.
13. Facilities will be appropriate and will be kept up-to-date. Equipment will require frequent replacement, more because of obsolescence than because of wear. The practice of leasing, rather than purchasing, equipment with regular replacement as obsolescence requires, may become widespread.
14. Schools will be open to students (including adults) for much longer hours and facilities such as library and documentation centre shall remain open even on the weekends.
15. All students will be provided course offerings that integrate academic and vocational subjects, and guidance programmes that will help them assess their interests, aptitude and career plans and relate this data to curriculum choices.

16. Technology will enter the office of the career counsellor and will take over his/her psychometric responsibilities, thus giving him/her more time to assist the career planner in identifying and dealing with other issues that may be getting in the way of attaining his/her career goal.
17. Career development theories will shift from a *structured* approach that considers career planning to be a once-in-a-lifetime event, towards an *unstructured* approach that acknowledges the need for recurring evaluations and decisions that take into consideration the career planners' changing life values and circumstances.
18. Career counsellors will need to become adept in dealing with both technology and transition. Specifically, they will need to become specialists in the use of self-instruction devices (*i.e.* career planning books, computer-assisted instructional software, interactive video programmes), so that they can guide their clients through educational programmes that teach them about the mechanics of career planning.
19. Guidance and career counsellors will specialize in assisting their clients to identify the job related transitional issues (*i.e.* job loss, job dissatisfaction, job re-structure) they are facing, and help them develop the coping skills and support systems they need in order to move through these transitional periods.
20. As job prospects dwindle for graduates of academic programmes, more students will choose to enroll in shorter-term vocational training programmes for non-professional occupations at community colleges or adult skill training centres.
21. The best administrators of technical-vocational programmes will be the persons whose professional qualifications have been augmented with personal experience in non-teaching careers related to the occupations being taught. Such administrators shall become active students of the vocations represented in their institution and will associate themselves enthusiastically with workers and leaders in these areas.

SUMMARY

This chapter examines the future of technical-vocational education. It is predicted that this phase of education will continue to be a part of

secondary education and not deferred to post-secondary level as believed by some. Further, the world of work will be readily different compared to what it is today, mainly due to automation and other socio-economical changes. The meaning of these trends for technical-vocational education is discussed and several important features of the future programmes of technical-vocational education are described.

INDEX